MCSE CoursePrep ExamGuide/StudyGuide Exam #70-216

Implementing and Administering a Microsoft Windows 2000 Network Infrastructure

COURSE TECHNOLOGY
THOMSON LEARNING™

Australia • Canada • Mexico • Singapore • Spain • United Kingdom • United States

COURSE TECHNOLOGY

THOMSON LEARNING™

MCSE CoursePrep ExamGuide and ***MCSE CoursePrep StudyGuide*** are published by Course Technology.

Managing Editor
Stephen Solomon

Senior Vice President, Publisher
Kristen Duerr

Production Editor
Brooke Albright, Trillium Project Management

Developmental Editor/Product Manager
Dave George

Associate Product Manager
Elizabeth Wessen

Editorial Assistant
Nick Lombardi

Marketing Manager
Toby Shelton

Text Designer
GEX Publishing Services

Cover Designer
Elizabeth Young

Printed in Canada

1 2 3 4 5 WC 03 02 01 00

For more information, contact Course Technology, 25 Thomson Place, Boston, Massachusetts, 02210.

Or find us on the World Wide Web at: www.course.com

ISBN 0-619-01503-9

ISBN 0-619-03506-4

TABLE OF CONTENTS

PREFACE

The *MCSE CoursePrep ExamGuide* and *MCSE CoursePrep StudyGuide* are the very best tools to use to prepare for exam day. These products are intended to be used with the core "Guide to" book, *MCSE Guide to Microsoft Windows 2000 Networking* (ISBN 0-619-01645-0), written by Kelly Caudle and Walter Glenn, and published by Course Technology. The *CoursePrep ExamGuide* and *CoursePrep StudyGuide* provide you ample opportunity to practice, drill, and rehearse for the exam!

CoursePrep ExamGuide

The *MCSE CoursePrep ExamGuide for Exam #70-216* (ISBN 0-619-03506-4) provides the essential information you need to master each exam objective. The *CoursePrepExamGuide* devotes an entire two-page spread to each certification objective for the exam, helping you understand the objective and giving you the bottom-line information—what you really need to know. Memorize these facts and bulleted points before heading into the exam. In addition, there are several practice test questions for each objective on the right-hand page. That's hundreds of questions to help you practice for the exam! The *CoursePrep ExamGuide* provides the exam fundamentals and gets you up to speed quickly. If you are seeking even more opportunity to practice and prepare, we recommend that you consider our total solution, the *CoursePrep StudyGuide*, which is described below.

CoursePrep StudyGuide

For those really serious about certification, we offer an even more robust solution—the *MCSE CoursePrep StudyGuide for Exam #70-216* (ISBN 0-619-01503-9). This offering includes all of the same quality material you get with the *CoursePrep ExamGuide*, including the unique two-page spread, the bulleted memorization points, and the practice questions. In addition, you receive a password valid for six months of practice on CoursePrep, a dynamic test preparation tool. The password is found in an envelope in the back cover of the *CoursePrep StudyGuide*. CoursePrep is a Web-based pool of hundreds of sample test questions. CoursePrep exam simulation software mimics the exact exam environment. The CoursePrep software is flexible and allows you to practice in several ways as you master the material. Choose from Certification Mode to experience actual exam-day conditions, or Study Mode to request answers and explanations to practice questions. Custom Mode lets you set the options for the practice test, including number of questions, content coverage, and ability to request answers and explanation. Follow the instructions on the inside back cover to access the exam simulation software. To see a demo of this dynamic test preparation tool, go to www.courseprep.com.

FEATURES

The *MCSE CoursePrep ExamGuide* and *MCSE CoursePrep StudyGuide* include the following features:

Detailed coverage of the certification objectives in a unique two-page spread. Study strategically by really focusing on the MCSE certification objectives. To enable you to do this, a two-page spread is devoted to each certification objective. The left-hand page provides the critical facts you need, while the right-hand page features practice questions relating to that objective. You'll find the certification objectives and sub-objectives clearly listed in the upper-left corner of each spread.

An overview of each objective is provided in the ***Understanding the Objective*** section. Next, ***What You Really Need to Know*** lists bulleted, succinct core facts, skills, and concepts about the objective. Memorizing these facts will be important for your success when taking the exam. ***Objectives on the Job*** places the objective in an industry perspective, and tells you how you can expect to incorporate the objective at work. This section also provides troubleshooting information.

Practice Test Questions on each right-hand page help you prepare for the exam by testing your skills, identifying your strengths and weaknesses, and demonstrating the subject matter you will face on the exam and how it will be tested. These questions are written in a similar fashion to real MCSE exam questions. The questions test your knowledge of the objectives described on the left-hand page and also the information in the *MCSE Guide to Microsoft Windows 2000 Networking*. Answers to the practice test questions are found at the back of this guide.

Glossary of Acronyms and Abbreviations: The world of networking, perhaps more than any other computer-related discipline, uses a language all its own, which is comprised largely of acronyms. You will find a complete list of all acronyms used in this guide, along with their meanings, at the back of the book.

For more information: If you require more information about networking concepts in general, or MCSE exam objectives in particular, please see *MCSE Guide to Microsoft Windows 2000 Networking*, by Kelly Caudle and Walter Glenn (Course Technology, 2001).

Section 1

Installing, Configuring, Managing, Monitoring, and Troubleshooting DNS in a Windows 2000 Network Infrastructure

OBJECTIVES

1.1 Install and configure DNS

DNS • FQDN

UNDERSTANDING THE OBJECTIVE

DNS is the foundation of a name resolution solution for a network, and is a required component for Active Directory. DNS is used both on the Internet and private **IP** networks.

WHAT YOU REALLY NEED TO KNOW

- **DNS** is a mechanism used to resolve human-friendly domain names into IP addresses.
- DNS can only be deployed on TCP/IP-based networks.
- The DNS service itself can only be installed on a Windows 2000 Server.
- Domain namespace is a hierarchical structure.
- The word "root" is at the top of the structure and is represented as a period.
- Below the root, top-level domain names are represented by an organizational type, such as .com, .org, .gov, .edu, or country codes such as .uk for the United Kingdom.
- Second-level domain names are registered to individuals or groups and may have multiple subdomain names. For example, microsoft.com is a second-level domain name and sales.microsoft.com is a subdomain.
- **FQDN** specifically identifies a host.
- Public domain names used on the Internet must be registered with a naming authority.
- Privately used domain names (e.g., within an intranet) do not need to be registered with any naming authority.
- DNS uses the FQDN to resolve a host's name to its IP address.
- DNS access is required for systems to access the Internet, but a local DNS is not strictly required.

OBJECTIVES ON THE JOB

As the number of systems on a network grows, it becomes increasingly important to deploy an addressing scheme that not only is easy to understand and use, but also offers unlimited scalability. DNS allows you to create a large, complex network that is still easy to use and navigate. The network operating system itself uses IP addresses (in a binary form), which are difficult for humans to remember but much easier to type in properly. But, through the use of FQDNs, which are very easy to remember and much easier to type in correctly, DNS handles the transformation of the FQDN to IP address automatically. DNS is often deployed on medium-sized or larger networks, on networks where Internet access is desired, and wherever Active Directory is used. For some networks connected to the Internet, an internal DNS server serves as a single access point for all internal systems to obtain name resolution services for external servers.

PRACTICE TEST QUESTIONS

1. **XYZ Corp's network is growing at a phenomenal rate. Each month, at least 40 new clients and three new servers are added. Users complain that locating resources by typing in IP addresses is becoming difficult. Each week, the resource department distributes a 15-page document that details each major network resource and the IP address of the system hosting the resource. Users must find the resource in the listing, then type in the IP address as part of a UNC name to reach resources.**

   As the network administrator, you are assigned the task of creating or deploying a new mechanism on the network that will simplify the resource location and access process. Which of the following solutions would require the least ongoing maintenance to support?
   a. WINS
   b. DHCP
   c. DNS
   d. HOSTS files on each system
2. **Which of the following conditions must be met for your choice of solution to be properly deployed? Keep in mind that your network is private. (Choose all that apply.)**
   a. All systems must be running Windows 2000.
   b. You must be running a TCP/IP-based network.
   c. A Windows 2000 Server system is available.
   d. You must have a publicly registered domain name.
3. **Active Directory must be present for DNS to be used.**
   a. True
   b. False
4. **The domain name microsoft.com can be labeled as a ______.**
   a. top-level domain
   b. root domain
   c. second-level domain
   d. sub-domain
5. **DNS is absolutely required on all systems connecting to the Internet.**
   a. True
   b. False
6. **DNS is scalable to what level?**
   a. 100 systems
   b. 1000 systems
   c. 16,000 systems
   d. Unlimited

OBJECTIVES

1.2 Install the DNS Server Service

DNS • HOST SYSTEM • TCP/IP SETTINGS

UNDERSTANDING THE OBJECTIVE

DNS is a service that can be installed on Windows 2000 Server. DNS installation is a simple process and can be performed during the initial installation of Windows 2000 Server, manually at any time, or by the Active Directory installation routine.

WHAT YOU REALLY NEED TO KNOW

- DNS can only be installed on a Windows 2000 Server using **TCP/IP**.
- The host system must have a static IP address.
- The host system should also have its DNS host name and domain name defined on the DNS tab of the Advanced TCP/IP Settings dialog box. The DNS host name is the computer's name.
- DNS is configured, by default, to accept updates from DHCP and to communicate with other DNS servers in the local domain.
- Further configuration is necessary for real-world use of DNS, which includes creating and managing zones.

OBJECTIVES ON THE JOB

DNS is used throughout the Internet to allow humans easier access to myriad resources. Through the use of FQDNs, computer users can type a simple **URL** and have instant access to anything on the Internet. The installation of DNS is a fairly common occurrence on TCP/IP networks. The DNS service can be installed during the initial installation, during an installation of Active Directory, or anytime desired through the Add/Remove Programs applet or the Network and Dial-up Connections tool. Installing DNS does not require a reboot (however, when installed along with Active Directory, a reboot is required by **AD**). Once DNS is installed, it immediately begins working for the local domain. DNS must be present on every domain controller, because it is an essential component of Active Directory. DNS is the foundation of a name resolution solution, which can simplify the process of locating and accessing resources on any network. DNS can be configured to interact with DHCP, **WINS**, and Windows 2000 to provide dynamic updates to its domain name-to-IP address mapping table.

PRACTICE TEST QUESTIONS

1. **When installing DNS, which of the following actions should be taken? (Choose all that apply.)**
   a. Install WINS.
   b. Define the host's DNS host name and domain name on the DNS tab of the Advanced TCP/IP Settings dialog box.
   c. Define a static IP address for the host.
   d. Install Active Directory.
2. **DNS can be installed on any Windows 2000 system.**
   a. True
   b. False
3. **Once DNS is installed, a zone must be configured before it will function.**
   a. True
   b. False
4. **When can DNS be installed? (Choose all that apply.)**
   a. During the initial installation
   b. During the Active Directory installation process
   c. Anytime after initial installation
   d. While in Disaster Recovery mode
5. **Which tool can be used to install DNS? (Choose all that apply.)**
   a. Network and Dial-up Connections tool
   b. Active Directory Users and Computers tool
   c. Add/Remove Programs applet
   d. System applet
6. **When DNS is installed manually, a reboot is not required.**
   a. True
   b. False
7. **In relation to Active Directory, DNS can be installed ______. (Choose all that apply.)**
   a. before the installation of Active Directory is launched
   b. on a different system on the network than the system that hosts Active Directory
   c. after the installation of Active Directory is complete
   d. during the installation of Active Directory

OBJECTIVES

1.3 Configure a root name server

ROOT NAME DNS SERVER • PRIVATE DOMAIN TREE

UNDERSTANDING THE OBJECTIVE

A root name DNS server is needed for any private domain tree. A root name DNS server defines the top-level domain names.

WHAT YOU REALLY NEED TO KNOW

- A root name server is required in every private domain tree.
- A root name server is not required if you have access to a root name server in another connected network (for example, the Internet). However, using a pre-existing root name server requires that you comply with its configuration limitations and conventions.
- Creating a root name server is the same process as creating a zone (see Objective 1.4 for information about zones).
- A root name server zone always has the name of "." (a period).
- A root name server is always a primary DNS server. A secondary DNS server obtains its copy of the zone information from another secondary server or from the primary DNS server.
- The root name server is created automatically when Active Directory is installed on the first domain controller, establishing a new domain.
- Use the DNS tool (in Administrative Tools) to manually create a root name server.

OBJECTIVES ON THE JOB

A root name server is required to establish a DNS service in a new private domain tree. Active Directory automatically creates a root name server on the first domain controller used to establish a new domain tree. Root name servers cannot have forwarders defined, because they are the final authority for all domains underneath them.

PRACTICE TEST QUESTIONS

1. **What is the valid name for the primary zone on a root name server?**
   a. dns.dns
   b. root.dns
   c. .
   d. root
2. **What is the default name of the zone file for the root name server's primary zone?**
   a. dns.dns
   b. root.dns
   c. .
   d. root
3. **The root server zone is automatically created by Active Directory when a new domain tree is established.**
   a. True
   b. False
4. **Every private domain tree requires its own root domain server.**
   a. True
   b. False
5. **Which of the following statements is true? (Choose all that apply.)**
   a. A root server is identified by its root zone ".".
   b. Creating a root domain zone involves the same process as creating any zone.
   c. Two or more domain servers are required in every domain tree.
   d. A root domain server can forward queries to other DNS servers.
6. **Which of the following is defined by a root name domain server?**
   a. Subdomains
   b. FQDNs
   c. Second-level domains
   d. Top-level domains
7. **A root domain zone is what type of zone? (Choose all that apply.)**
   a. Primary zone
   b. Secondary zone
   c. Reverse lookup zone
   d. Forward lookup zone

OBJECTIVES

1.4 Configure zones

DNS ZONES • NAMESPACES

UNDERSTANDING THE OBJECTIVE

A zone is a logically defined portion of a domain DNS namespace or multiple domains' DNS namespaces. Zones must be created and managed to divide a network into manageable DNS namespaces.

WHAT YOU REALLY NEED TO KNOW

- A zone is the designated source of information about a domain name.
- A DNS server has the ability to resolve FQDNs within a zone.
- A single DNS server can manage one or more zones.
- Information about a zone and all domain names within a zone are stored in a zone file on the DNS server. Typically, the zone file is named <domain_name>.dns.
- There are three zone types:
  - Standard primary – the master zone where changes can be recorded; data is stored in a text-only zone file.
  - Standard secondary – a read-only backup copy of the master zone used for load distributing; data is stored in a text-only zone file.
  - Active Directory Integrated – zone data is stored in Active Directory; AD manages all data updates in the zone.
- Zones can be either forward lookup or reverse lookup. Forward lookup zones resolve FQDNs into IP addresses. Reverse lookup zones resolve IP addresses into FQDNs.

OBJECTIVES ON THE JOB

The use of zones grants you flexibility in the design of your network. Because a single DNS server can manage the zones for one or more domains, you don't need a DNS server in each and every domain and subdomain. A single DNS server can host a single zone file, multiple zone files, or no zone files. If workload is sufficient, you can create secondary zone files on additional DNS servers to spread out the workload. You should create a unique zone for sections of a network that interact often (for example, clients and related servers) or by departments or other pre-existing logical divisions.

PRACTICE TEST QUESTIONS

1. **ZYG Corp. has a domain tree with zyg.com as the root, or parent, domain and sales.zyg.com, research.zyg.com, and misc.zyg.com as its three child domains. The DNS server in the zyg.com domain is configured with a standard primary zone, which covers all host names and domain names within these four domains. There are plans to further expand the current domain tree with at least four new child domains.**

   Upper management requested that performance over all network activities remain good, and that the additional workload not be allowed to cause performance delays. In addition to adding more hardware, installing new servers, and updating routers and NICs to 100 MB capacity, what additional step should you take?
    a. Create a new zone for the three new child domains.
    b. Deploy a DNS server in each child domain with a standard secondary zone.
    c. Collapse all current child domains into the parent domain.
    d. Install a WINS server in each child domain.
2. **A few months after you deployed your solution, you wish to spread the workload of zone management to other capable network administrators. What is the next step in the process of granting other users management control over distinct areas of the network?**
    a. Create an organizational unit for each domain that contains only those objects within a single domain.
    b. Create a standard primary zone file for the entire network on each DNS server.
    c. Create a standard primary zone file for each distinct domain.
    d. Rename the root zone name to zyg.com.
3. **A single DNS server can support multiple zones.**
    a. True
    b. False
4. **A DNS server must have at least one zone defined.**
    a. True
    b. False
5. **Which of the following statements is true?**
    a. All standard primary zones must have a standard secondary zone.
    b. A DNS server can only resolve a domain name if it is contained within a zone.
    c. The zone file name must match the zone name.
    d. Zone updates must be defined even for Active Directory integrated zones.
6. **A reverse lookup zone is used to resolve ______.**
    a. FQDNs into IP addresses
    b. MAC addresses into IP addresses
    c. FQDNs into MAC addresses
    d. IP addresses into FQDNs

OBJECTIVES

1.5 Configure a caching-only server

DNS CACHING-ONLY SERVER • FORWARDER • QUERY

UNDERSTANDING THE OBJECTIVE

A DNS caching-only server does not perform name resolution itself. Rather, it forwards resolution queries to other DNS servers, and then maintains a list (cache) of the results. Any future requests for the same resolution are resolved from cache.

WHAT YOU REALLY NEED TO KNOW

- A caching-only server does not maintain zone files.
- A caching-only server forwards queries to other DNS servers and then maintains a list of the most active query results.
- The list of processed queries is maintained in memory; thus, adding more memory to a caching-only server increases the amount of resolved queries it can retain.
- You create a caching-only server in a two-step process. First, install DNS on Windows 2000 Server, but don't define any forward or reverse lookup zones. Second, define a forwarder.
- Forwarders can be defined on any DNS server, except a root server. On DNS servers that host zone files, only those queries unable to be resolved within their own local zone files are forwarded to other DNS servers.

OBJECTIVES ON THE JOB

Caching-only servers are often deployed in situations where a domain or subnet is separated from the primary network via a low-bandwidth link. A caching-only server stores lookup data locally and is therefore able to quickly resolve addresses without issuing a new DNS query every time the same address is requested (which wastes additional bandwidth over a slow link). Additionally, a caching-only server does not maintain any zone files, thus it does not participate in zone transfers, which results in even less wasted bandwidth. Usually, only large organizations and **ISPs** employ caching-only servers.

PRACTICE TEST QUESTIONS

1. **A DNS server cannot have zones defined locally.**
   a. True
   b. False
2. **Which of the following statements is true of caching-only servers? (Choose all that apply.)**
   a. They retain the most active resolutions in memory.
   b. They do not have locally defined zones.
   c. They help reduce workload on other DNS servers.
   d. They do not participate in zone transfers.
3. **The number of active queries retained by a caching-only server is directly related to the amount of memory installed on the host system.**
   a. True
   b. False
4. **Which of the following DNS servers can have forwarders defined? (Choose all that apply.)**
   a. DNS servers with no forward or reverse lookup zones
   b. DNS servers with forward lookup zones
   c. DNS servers with reverse lookup zones
   d. DNS root servers
5. **To how many DNS servers can a forwarder send queries?**
   a. 1
   b. 2
   c. 4
   d. As many as you define
6. **A caching-only server performs local resolutions.**
   a. True
   b. False
7. **A caching-only server should be used ______. (Choose all that apply.)**
   a. when other DNS servers are overburdened
   b. when a remote domain or subnet is connected over a slow link
   c. when you want to maintain a fault-tolerant backup of the DNS zone files
   d. when you want to resolve NetBIOS names into IP addresses

OBJECTIVES

1.6 Configure a DNS client

DNS CLIENT • HOSTS FILE • DHCP

UNDERSTANDING THE OBJECTIVE

Clients can take advantage of the services offered by a DNS system only if they are configured to do so. Client configuration takes place through the TCP/IP properties on their local system. The primary configuration setting that must be made is to provide the IP address of the DNS server.

WHAT YOU REALLY NEED TO KNOW

- Clients can be configured to use DNS through DHCP or through direct manual configuration (in the cases of clients using static IP addresses.
- Each client must be configured to send queries to a DNS server by providing the DNS server's IP address.
- On Windows 2000 systems, the DNS configuration settings are on the General tab of the TCP/IP Properties dialog box.
- On Windows 95/98/SE/ME systems, the DNS configuration settings are on the DNS tab of the TCP/IP Properties dialog box.
- In most cases, only a single primary DNS server must be defined, but if a secondary DNS server is available, it can be listed as well.
- On networks where DNS servers are not available, HOSTS files can be used. A HOSTS file is a static text form of the DNS database that a system can use to locally resolve domain names into IP addresses. HOSTS files are text files that must be managed manually and should be stored in the *windowsroot*\system3\drivers\etc folder.
- When a HOSTS file is present, it is used to attempt a query resolution before a DNS server is contacted.
- If your subnet or domain is using a DNS caching server locally, be sure to provide its IP address in the client configuration instead of a zone hosting DNS server.

OBJECTIVES ON THE JOB

The purpose of installing DNS servers on a network is to grant clients and other systems the ability to use them to resolve FQDNs into IP addresses. Each system that uses DNS must be configured to send resolution queries directly to the DNS server via its IP address. For dynamically configured systems using DHCP, the DHCP server can provide this information. Otherwise, each static system must be manually configured with the IP address of the DNS server. HOSTS files were used for FQDN resolution before DNS servers were created. They are still supported today and used on smaller networks. But, because they require manual upkeep, they become cumbersome as a network grows.

PRACTICE TEST QUESTIONS

1. **All clients are automatically configured to send queries to DNS servers.**
   a. True
   b. False
2. **Which clients must be manually configured to use DNS servers? (Choose all that apply.)**
   a. Those using DHCP
   b. Those using WINS
   c. Those with static IP addresses
   d. Those without a HOSTS file
3. **The HOSTS file is an automatically updated component of a DNS server.**
   a. True
   b. False
4. **When configuring clients to use DNS, which configuration setting is required?**
   a. DNS server's host name
   b. IP address of DNS server
   c. Subnet mask of DNS server
   d. Domain name where DNS server resides
5. **Most Windows operating systems can have which of the following DNS-related configuration settings defined? (Choose all that apply.)**
   a. Primary DNS server
   b. Secondary DNS server
   c. DNS server use priority
   d. DNS server query response timeout
6. **A HOSTS file is stored in ______.**
   a. a user's local profile directory
   b. the main Windows directory
   c. the Program Files directory
   d. the system32\drivers\etc subdirectory of the main Windows directory
7. **Which configuration offers the fastest performance for query resolutions?**
   a. Configure the client to use a DNS server.
   b. Place a HOSTS file on the client and configure it to use a DNS server.
   c. Configure the client to use a caching DNS server.
   d. Configure the client to use a primary and a secondary DNS server.

OBJECTIVES

1.7 Configure zones for dynamic updates

DYNAMIC DNS • RESOURCE RECORD

UNDERSTANDING THE OBJECTIVE

Windows 2000 supports Dynamic DNS, which can be automatically updated by A and PTR resource records sent to the DNS server when a system boots. The dynamic update ability of DNS is not enabled by default. Dynamic updates greatly reduce the amount of work involved in maintaining current DNS zones.

WHAT YOU REALLY NEED TO KNOW

- Dynamic DNS is not enabled by default. Use the DNS tool (in Administrative Tools) to enable DNS.
- Once Dynamic DNS is enabled, systems can automatically register themselves with DNS when booting using an A or PTR resource record.
- Dynamic updates are enabled by changing the Allow dynamic updates setting for a zone from “Only Secure Updates” to “Yes”.
- The settings for the Allow dynamic updates pull-down list are: No, Yes, and Only Secure Updates. These settings correlate to Disable, Enable, and Enable only for authorized clients in an Active Directory integrated zone. Note: The Yes setting is not considered secure because any system can register DNS data.
- You can further configure the interaction for Dynamic DNS with DHCP.
- Windows 2000 clients can be configured to send updates to DNS.

OBJECTIVES ON THE JOB

Allowing your network clients to update the DNS zone as they boot greatly reduces the amount of administrative overhead required to maintain an up-to-date DNS system. However, dynamic updates are only secure when Active Directory manages the update procedure. The only other secure setting is to prevent dynamic updates from occurring. Otherwise, any client can submit false DNS information and corrupt your DNS system. In most networks where physical security is maintained, this will not be a problem, but it is something to be aware of. In addition to simply configuring DNS servers to accept dynamic updates, you must also configure DHCP and/or clients to send the updates to the DNS servers. Only Windows 2000 clients can send this information directly to DNS, but non-Windows 2000 clients can register their settings with DNS through DHCP.

PRACTICE TEST QUESTIONS

1. **Dynamic DNS is enabled by default.**
    a. True
    b. False
2. **Which type of resource record submitted by a client is used to update dynamic DNS? (Choose all that apply.)**
    a. A
    b. BOOTP
    c. ARP
    d. PTR
3. **DNS must always be manually updated.**
    a. True
    b. False
4. **Which DNS server setting, in relation to dynamic updates, is secure? (Choose all that apply.)**
    a. No
    b. Yes
    c. Only Secure Updates
5. **By what means can DNS be updated? (Choose all that apply.)**
    a. Active Directory integrated
    b. DHCP
    c. Directly from Windows 2000 clients
    d. Directly from non-Windows 2000 clients
6. **What type of client can have its DNS information automatically updated? (Choose all that apply.)**
    a. DHCP client
    b. Windows 2000 client
    c. Non-Windows 2000 client
    d. Non-TCP/IP client
7. **Windows 2000 clients can send DNS update information directly to a DNS server.**
    a. True
    b. False

OBJECTIVES

1.8 Test the DNS server service

IPCONFIG • NSLOOKUP • DNSCMD

UNDERSTANDING THE OBJECTIVE

DNS is a behind-the-scenes service as long as it is running properly. Windows 2000 includes several tools that can be used to verify the functionality of DNS and to detect problems should they exist.

WHAT YOU REALLY NEED TO KNOW

- Use the **IPCONFIG** tool to verify DNS configurations from the client and server.
- Run the command ipconfig /all at the command line to display a detailed report of IP configuration. The important items to review in regard to DNS in the report are "DNS Suffix Search List" and "DNS Servers." These should match the settings defined when IP was configured.
- The command ipconfig /registerdns causes the system's DNS information to be registered with the DNS server. Any errors with this process are recorded in Event Viewer.
- The command ipconfig /displaydns displays the client's DNS revolver cache. The command ipconfig /flushdns clears the cache.
- Use the **NSLOOKUP** tool to directly interrogate the DNS server. NSLOOKUP can extract reports that include information such as the domain or host names stored in the DNS server and their respective IP addresses.
- NSLOOKUP has two modes of operation: interactive and non-interactive.
- Use the **DNSCMD** tool, a command-line version of the DNS **GUI** tool, to check registration of DNS resource records.

OBJECTIVES ON THE JOB

Verifying that DNS servers and clients are configured and working properly is an important final step before allowing your DNS solution to be employed on your production network. Windows 2000 DNS has many dynamic features that enable it to maintain a current table of domain-name-to-IP-address mappings. However, configuration of clients and the DNS servers themselves are crucial to the ongoing functionality of this service.

PRACTICE TEST QUESTIONS

1. **The network at HSO Corp. has decided to install a DNS server. After deploying a primary zone and two secondary zone servers to distribute the load of name resolution, they attempt to configure the clients to use DNS. What tool should be used to check that the correct DNS suffix is defined and the appropriate DNS servers are set on each client?**
    a. ROUTE
    b. IPCONFIG
    c. NSLOOKUP
    d. NET
2. **After using this tool, the system administrator discovered that the wrong IP address was entered on every client. After painstakingly reconfiguring the IP address on each client, he wants to flush out any incorrect DNS information maintained by the client. Which tool should be used?**
    a. ROUTE
    b. IPCONFIG
    c. NSLOOKUP
    d. NET
3. **The NSLOOKUP tool can be used to extract the host-name-to-IP-address mapping table from a DNS server.**
    a. True
    b. False
4. **There are three tools that can be used to test DNS:**
    a. IPCONFIG
    b. NSLOOKUP
    c. DNSCMD

    Match the following statements with these tools (some items may be used more than once):
    1. Command-line tool
    2. View IP configuration of local system
    3. Interrogate DNS server
    4. Manage and configure DNS server
    5. View Local DNS cache
    6. Clear DNS cache
    7. Two modes of operation
5. **The IPCONFIG tool can be used to force a client system to register itself with DNS.**
    a. True
    b. False
6. **Which tool is designed for use in batch scripts to help administrators automate repetitive tasks?**
    a. IPCONFIG
    b. NSLOOKUP
    c. DNSCMD

OBJECTIVES

1.9 Implement a delegated zone for DNS

ZONE DELEGATIONS • NS RECORDS

UNDERSTANDING THE OBJECTIVE

Zone delegation is the process of assigning a DNS server to answer queries for a specific zone. This process is used to distribute DNS workload and to aid the direction of network traffic.

WHAT YOU REALLY NEED TO KNOW

- Zones can be delegated to primary or secondary DNS servers.
- Delegation is accomplished by adding an NS record to the zone file to define the authoritative DNS server for that zone.
- When a non-authoritative DNS server receives a query for a zone, it forwards that query to the DNS server listed in the NS record for that zone.
- Zone delegations are defined through the DNS utility's New Delegation Wizard, launched by issuing the New Delegation command from the Action menu when a zone is selected. You must provide the name of the domain to be delegated and the IP addresses of the DNS server(s) to become the authoritative servers for the zone.
- It is possible to add NS records directly to the text zone file. However, you must type the necessary data exactly as required by syntax.

OBJECTIVES ON THE JOB

Zone delegation is seen at its most extreme when a root or top-level domain DNS server must off-load the burden of responding to queries for all of the zones of its child domains. For example, the root server usually has zone delegations for .com. .org, .gov, and so forth to the DNS servers for those top-level domains. Likewise, the .com DNS server has zone delegations for myriad second-level domains, such as microsoft.com, lanw.com, ilearning.com, and cnet.com. Thus, the burden of query response is passed down the delegation hierarchy so only the authoritative DNS server for a zone must reply to queries regarding host names defined within its zones. Zone delegation should not be undertaken when you need to balance the workload that one or more DNS servers are carrying across additional, alternate, or newly deployed DNS servers. Zone delegation is not a form of a secondary server or even a caching-only server, but a method to push off query responses from one DNS server to another.

PRACTICE TEST QUESTIONS

1. **Which of the following must be provided when defining a zone delegation? (Choose all that apply.)**
   a. Name of the delegated domain
   b. IP address of the zone's DHCP server
   c. IP address of the DNS server to be authoritative over a zone
   d. Names of the reverse lookup zones
2. **How can zone delegations be created? (Choose all that apply.)**
   a. Manually editing the zone file
   b. Properly configuring clients to send queries to delegated DNS servers
   c. Using multicast scopes for all DNS servers
   d. Using the Delegation Wizard
3. **Zones can be delegated to primary or secondary DNS servers.**
   a. True
   b. False
4. **Root DNS servers and even top-level domain DNS servers are often configured to delegate zones to a child domain's DNS servers.**
   a. True
   b. False
5. **What is a benefit of zone delegation? (Choose all that apply.)**
   a. The workload of query response is more intelligently balanced.
   b. Clients receive a faster rate of query response.
   c. Queries are answered only by their authoritative zone.
   d. It enhances the number of clients than can be supported by a single DNS server.
6. **Zone delegation is enabled by default on child domains.**
   a. True
   b. False
7. **When a DNS server receives a query in a zone that has a zone delegation defined, what happens?**
   a. The DNS server breaks the query.
   b. The DNS server forwards the query to the authoritative DNS server.
   c. The DNS server replies to the query.
   d. The DNS server send out a broadcast that it is not the authority for the domain.

OBJECTIVES

1.10 Manually create DNS resource records

DNS RESOURCE RECORDS • EDITING ZONE FILES

UNDERSTANDING THE OBJECTIVE

While DNS, under Windows 2000, can be used with no manual configuration, you can choose to add or edit DNS resource records manually. Usually, adding resource records manually helps smooth migration and deployment processes by predefining new host name-to-IP-address relationships instead of waiting for the system to register itself upon booting.

WHAT YOU REALLY NEED TO KNOW

- DNS records can be added to a DNS server through two methods: Edit the zone file for the specific zone or use the DNS utility to edit the zone through the GUI.
- There is one exception: You cannot edit the zone file of an Active Directory integrated zone, because the zone data is stored within Active Directory and not in a text file.
- The DNS zone files are text, so any text editor, such as Notepad, can be used to view and alter their contents. The only issue you really need to be concerned about is the type of records contained within these files. See the Windows 2000 Server Help documentation under DNS Resource Records for complete details.
- Through the DNS GUI tool, zones can be easily edited, added, or deleted.

OBJECTIVES ON THE JOB

Managing DNS manually was the norm until the release of Windows 2000. With the advent of Dynamic DNS, which can receive updates from DHCP, Active Directory, and even directly from Windows 2000 systems, manual administration is greatly reduced. However, there are many instances in which manual editing is preferred to allow the network to magically configure itself. We highly recommend that you use the GUI, which prevents you from entering invalid data. But, if you are fully aware of the restrictions, syntax, layout, and parameters required by the zone file, you can edit it with any text editor.

PRACTICE TEST QUESTIONS

1. **DNS records can be managed only through Active Directory.**
   a. True
   b. False
2. **How can DNS records be altered? (Choose all that apply.)**
   a. Editing the text zone file
   b. Altering Active Directory
   c. Booting a properly configured Windows 2000 Professional client
   d. Configuring DHCP
   e. Through a NET command at the command prompt
   f. Using the DNS GUI tool
3. **DNS systems always allow dynamic updates from clients.**
   a. True
   b. False
4. **Manual updates of DNS records can occur through what means? (Choose all that apply.)**
   a. Editing the zone file with a text editor
   b. Booting a properly configured Windows 2000 server onto the network
   c. Using the DNS GUI tool
   d. Using the Computer Management tool in Administrative Tools
5. **Which of the following are valid record types that can be added to a zone file? (Choose all that apply.)**
   a. Host
   b. Alias
   c. Subnet
   d. Mail exchanger
   e. Delegation
   f. Organizational unit
   g. Domain
6. **Active Directory integrated zones have text-only zone files that can be manually edited with a text editor.**
   a. True
   b. False
7. **Which of the following actions can be performed during a manual zone file edit? (Choose all that apply.)**
   a. New record added
   b. Current record changed
   c. Existing record deleted
   d. Zone file altered from primary to secondary zone

OBJECTIVES

1.11 Manage DNS

RESOURCE RECORDS • BIND

UNDERSTANDING THE OBJECTIVE

Managing and maintaining DNS involves the procedures described within this entire section. They include configuring zones, creating and altering resource records, defining caching-only servers, configuring DNS clients, configuring zones for dynamic updates, configuring delegated zones, and troubleshooting problems.

WHAT YOU REALLY NEED TO KNOW

- There are several types of resource records used by DNS:
  - A (address, host): contains the host-name-to-IP-address relationship
  - NS (name server): lists the name servers that have authority over this zone (i.e., they host the zone file)
  - CNAME (canonical name): defines additional names for a host that already has an A record
  - MX (mail exchange): defines the location of the e-mail server used to support e-mail directed to users @*thisdomain*
  - SOA (start of authority): defines the system where the zone was originally defined
  - PTR (pointer): defines the reverse lookup mapping for a host
  - SRV (service): the resource record used by services to allow users to locate them via DNS
- Windows 2000 DNS can interact with non-Windows 2000 DNS as long as the system supports RFC 2052 SRV records and RFS 2136 Dynamic DNS.
- To deploy a non-Windows 2000 DNS system to support Active Directory requires a service such as **BIND** 8.2.2.2 or 9.0 for UNIX, which supports Active Directory.
- If Active Directory integrated zones are used, BIND can serve only as a secondary server.
- To include non-Windows 2000 DNS in zone transfers from an Active Directory integrated zone, add the DNS server's IP address to the Zone Transfers tab of that zone's Properties dialog box.

OBJECTIVES ON THE JOB

In most cases with Dynamic DNS under Windows 2000, after the zones are properly configured, there is little to no ongoing maintenance required. You can regularly perform tests from old and new clients to verify that mappings are still occurring properly, but there is little need to inspect and adjust DNS on a daily basis.

PRACTICE TEST QUESTIONS

1. **The following are the resource record types supported by Windows 2000 DNS:**
    a. A
    b. NS
    c. CNAME
    d. MX
    e. SOA
    f. SVR
    g. PTR

    Match these record types with the following definitions:
    1. Defines the location of the e-mail server used to support e-mail directed to users *@thisdomain*
    2. Lists the name servers that have authority over this zone (i.e., they host the zone file)
    3. The resource record used by services to allow users to locate them via DNS
    4. Defines additional names for a host that already has an A record
    5. Defines the system where the zone was originally defined
    6. Contains the host name to IP address relationship
    7. Defines the reverse lookup mapping for a host

2. **UNIX DNS servers can participate in maintaining the naming service for a Windows 2000-based domain using Active Directory.**
    a. True
    b. False

3. **If the Active Directory integrated zones are used, BIND serves only as a secondary server.**
    a. True
    b. False

4. **Managing a DNS system requires which of the following skills? (Choose all that apply.)**
    a. Configuring zones
    b. Scripting
    c. Creating and altering resource records
    d. Defining caching-only servers
    e. Using the route command
    f. Configuring DNS clients
    g. Configuring zones for dynamic updates
    h. Using BOOTP
    i. Configuring delegated zones
    j. Troubleshooting problems

5. **Active Directory integrated zones cannot send zone transfer updates to non-Windows 2000 DNS servers.**
    a. True
    b. False

OBJECTIVES

1.12 Monitor and troubleshoot DNS

MONITORING UTILITY • SYSTEM MONITOR • EVENT LOG • EVENT VIEWER

UNDERSTANDING THE OBJECTIVE

You can monitor a DNS server using several methods. The DNS utility itself offers a query verification and testing service. System Monitor can be used to view the performance metrics of the DNS system. Event Viewer can be used to view the contents of the DNS Server Event Log. The DNS service itself can record a log file.

WHAT YOU REALLY NEED TO KNOW

- The Monitoring tab on a DNS server's Properties dialog box, accessed through the DNS tool, can be used to test DNS. Your options are to manually test a simple query against the local DNS server and/or a recursive query against other DNS servers known by this server. You can also configure a repeated automatic test to occur at a defined interval (minimum 30 seconds). A window at the bottom of this dialog lists the PASS and FAIL status of each query.
- System Monitor can be used to view DNS service performance statistics. The DNS object offers over 50 counters related to the DNS service. You can discover specific information about what each counter measures by viewing the Explain window through the Add Counters dialog.
- The DNS Server Event Log can be viewed through Event Viewer. Event details related to the function, configuration, and errors of DNS are recorded in this log file. When DNS is functioning as expected, the few event details recorded are informative about normal updates and zone transfers. When DNS is not functioning properly, the event details should provide you with enough information to determine and resolve the problem.
- Each DNS server can record a log file of any and all activities it performs. You configure the log file on the Logging tab of the Properties dialog of the DNS server through the DNS utility. On this tab, you can select from a list of items to record in the log file: query, notify, update, questions, answers, send, receive, **UDP**, TCP, full packets, and write through. The dns.log file is stored in the main Windows directory in the \system32\dns folder. This log file is for debugging purposes, so it contains many system-level details.

OBJECTIVES ON THE JOB

DNS operates with little or no management or oversight, once properly configured. Monitoring DNS becomes necessary when name resolution problems occur. The monitoring capabilities included in the DNS utility itself, along with those native to the operating system, provide system administrators with a wide range of tools for tracking down problems. Although these tools are simple to use, they should be explored before a problem actually exists—practice makes perfect.

PRACTICE TEST QUESTIONS

1. **GOB Corp.'s network consists of 4000 clients and 250 servers. Most of the systems use Windows 2000 Professional or Windows 2000 Server, but a few Windows NT 4.0 Workstation and Windows 98 clients are still present on the network. All clients are configured to use local DNS to resolve host names. Last weekend, the network administrator performed system maintenance, which included upgrading a few clients to Windows 2000 Professional, adding additional hard drives to a few servers, installing additional network application software, and updating drivers for video adapters and printers, along with numerous other minor adjustments or setting configurations. On Monday morning, many users reported that a DNS error occurred every time they attempted to access the corporation's internal Web site. Which of the following is the best first step in diagnosing and troubleshooting this problem?**
   a. Start recording performance data for the DNS service through System Monitor.
   b. Reboot all servers on the network.
   c. Perform several test queries from the DNS server.
   d. Delete and re-create the zone files.
2. **You complete the first step you selected in Question 1. You then discover that DNS is not responding to any queries. Which of the following is the next best step to take?**
   a. Start recording performance data for the DNS service through System Monitor.
   b. Start a DNS server log file.
   c. View the DNS Server Event Log.
   d. Transform all zones into Active Directory integrated zones.
3. **Which of the following is a mechanism used to view DNS activity? (Choose all that apply.)**
   a. System Monitor
   b. Event Viewer
   c. Device Manager
   d. Service Log file
   e. Active Directory Domains and Trusts
   f. Query Tests
4. **The performance metrics of the DNS service can be recorded by the System Monitor for inclusion in your regular baseline comparison procedures.**
   a. True
   b. False
5. **The DNS server's own log file capabilities record events such as queries, updates, and answers to the DNS server log file viewed through Event Viewer.**
   a. True
   b. False

Section 2

Installing, Configuring, Managing, Monitoring, and Troubleshooting DHCP in a Windows 2000 Network Infrastructure

OBJECTIVES

2.1 Install and configure DHCP

DHCPDISCOVER • DHCPOFFER • DHCPREQUEST • DHCPACK • IP LEASE • IPCONFIG

UNDERSTANDING THE OBJECTIVE

DHCP is a service used on networks to automatically configure the TCP/IP settings on systems (usually clients) as they boot. DHCP simplifies client configuration by retaining all IP settings in a centralized location. DHCP ensures that address conflicts are not caused by manual configuration errors.

WHAT YOU REALLY NEED TO KNOW

- DHCP can be used to assign IP addresses, subnet masks, default gateways, DNS servers, and WINS servers to clients.
- When a new client boots, it broadcasts a DHCPDISCOVER message to the entire network. This message includes the NIC's **MAC** address. The DHCP server intercepts this message and replies with a DHCPOFFER message directed to the client's MAC address. This message contains an IP address, subnet, lease length, and IP address of the DHCP server. The client responds with a DHCPREQUEST message to accept the offered lease. The DHCP server returns a final DHCPACK to acknowledge a successful lease.
- If a DHCP server fails to respond, the client rebroadcasts its DHCPDISCOVER message in two, four, eight, and 16 seconds. If there's still no response, the client automatically selects an address from the reserved range of 169.254.0.1 to 169.254.255.254 and continues to rebroadcast every five minutes.
- IP configurations are leased to clients. The client must renew or release the IP configuration before the leasing period expires. The DHCP client attempts to renew the lease when half the lease period has expired by transmitting a DHCPREQUEST message. If not acknowledged, it repeats the message when half the remaining lease period has passed. The DHCP server can respond with a lease extension or a new set of configuration settings.
- DHCP clients can use ipconfig /renew and ipconfig /release to force actions.
- Configure DHCP clients by setting their TCP/IP properties to Obtain an IP address automatically, or a similar setting. DNS servers can be manually configured on the clients; all other configuration takes place on the DHCP server.

OBJECTIVES ON THE JOB

DHCP allows for easy and automatic network configuration. DHCP simplifies client configuration and allows a smaller number of IP addresses to serve a larger number of transient clients (i.e., clients that are not online at the same time). For example, if only 29 out of 100 clients connect to the network at any given time, only 20 addresses in a DHCP scope for those clients are required, instead of the 100 required by manual configuration. This reduces the cost of IP addresses leased from a third party.

PRACTICE TEST QUESTIONS

1. **Borg Inc. has three technical support teams. Each team of 30 employees works an eight-hour shift, allowing the phones to be fully manned 24 hours a day. Support employees use company-provided notebook computers, which are connected to the office LAN during the employees' shifts and are taken home for study and continued education when the shifts are over. The teams work in 30 individual cubicles; one worker must disconnect and leave before the next shift's worker can connect to the LAN.**

   Due to the requirements of technical support, each of the notebook systems, when connected to the network, needs a public IP address. The leasing agreement between Borg Inc. and its ISP indicates that each public IP address costs $150 per month.

   New budgetary restrictions have limited the technical support ISP budget to $5000. Assume the entire budget can be spent on IP address leasing. Which of the following scenarios represents the best solution to keep costs low?
   a. Fire at least 20 people from each of the three support teams.
   b. Force the support teams to work in groups of three and share a notebook.
   c. Divide the support teams into groups of three, and deploy a proxy server system for each group.
   d. Deploy DHCP and use a scope of 30 public addresses.

2. **Borg Inc. discovered that, during the first and last 30 minutes of each shift, the quality of technical support is greatly diminished. It is determined that the anticipation of the end of the shift and the settling-in time affect the teams' performance. Thus, a proposal has been put forth to stagger the support staff. Six teams of 15 members each work eight-hour shifts, staggered at four-hour intervals, so only half the total number of technical support workers at any time are affected by the shift-change phenomena. Can DHCP still manage this type of situation?**
   a. Yes, with no change to existing configurations
   b. Yes, if all clients are assigned a static address
   c. Yes, if an additional 15 IP addresses are leased from the ISP
   d. No, DHCP cannot manage this type of situation.

3. **DNS and DHCP are mutually exclusive.**
   a. True
   b. False

4. **I am about to physically disconnect the network cable from the NIC on my client system. The client is configured to use DHCP. Other clients are waiting to use the IP address configuration that I am currently using. I will continue to use my computer after I disconnect from the network. Which of the following is the smartest course of action?**
   a. Issue the ipconfig /renew command.
   b. Issue the ipconfig /release command.
   c. Issue the net /disconnect command.
   d. Use the Start, Shutdown command to log off.

OBJECTIVES

2.2 Install the DHCP server service

DHCP SERVICE • SCOPE

UNDERSTANDING THE OBJECTIVE

The DHCP service is not a default component. It can be installed either during the initial installation of Windows 2000 Server or anytime afterward. Once a DHCP server is installed and configured, it can serve a wide number of clients.

WHAT YOU REALLY NEED TO KNOW

- DHCP is a service that must be installed on a Windows 2000 Server using TCP/IP.
- The host system must have a static IP address, subnet mask, and default gateway defined.
- Once the DHCP service is installed, a scope must be defined and authorized before the DHCP service can lease IP configurations to clients. The requirement for authorization is a Windows 2000 issue; non-Windows 2000 DHCP servers do not require authorization.
- To authorize a DHCP server, you must be a member of the Enterprise Admins group.
- Unauthorized Windows 2000 DHCP servers record an error in the Event Log and the DHCP service is disabled.

OBJECTIVES ON THE JOB

Installing DHCP on a Windows 2000 domain network is often an intelligent way to reduce client configuration overhead. A DHCP server hosted by Windows 2000 Server can provide automated IP configuration data for a wide range of clients, including Windows 2000, Windows NT, Windows 98, Windows 95, Windows for Workgroups 3.11 with Microsoft TCP/IP-32, MS-DOS with Microsoft Network Client version 3.0 and the real-mode TCP/IP driver, Microsoft LAN Manager 2.2c, and many non-Microsoft operating systems that support TCP/IP.

PRACTICE TEST QUESTIONS

1. **Which of the following is a requirement for deploying DHCP on Windows 2000? (Choose all that apply.)**
    a. Windows 2000 Server
    b. DNS servers
    c. Static IP address and subnet mask
    d. NWLink
    e. Default gateway
2. **DHCP is a default component of Windows 2000 Server.**
    a. True
    b. False
3. **To authorize a DHCP server, you must be a member of the Enterprise Admins group.**
    a. True
    b. False
4. **What must be done after Windows 2000 Server is installed so that IP configurations are automatically assigned to clients? (Choose all that apply.)**
    a. Define at least one scope.
    b. Install the DHCP service.
    c. Deploy DNS.
    d. Authorize the DHCP service.
5. **Which type of system requires authorization?**
    a. Windows 2000 Server DHCP servers
    b. Windows NT Server DHCP servers
    c. Non-Microsoft server DHCP servers
    d. Windows 2000 DHCP clients
6. **Which of the following are benefits of DHCP? (Choose all that apply.)**
    a. Integration with WINS
    b. Ease of network configuration
    c. Centralized client configuration management
    d. Support for a wide range of clients
7. **Unauthorized Windows DHCP servers continue to respond to clients by providing them with configurations.**
    a. True
    b. False

OBJECTIVES

2.3 Create DHCP scopes

SCOPES

UNDERSTANDING THE OBJECTIVE

A scope is a defined range of IP addresses that can be leased to clients. DHCP is based around scopes. Scopes can be large blocks of IP addresses or complex definitions with exclusions, reservations, and advanced options.

WHAT YOU REALLY NEED TO KNOW

- DHCP works through the use of scopes (IP address pools). If a free address is available within a scope, it can be assigned to a requesting client.
- A scope can also be used to provide clients with a default gateway address, DNS server addresses, WINS server addresses, and other configuration settings. These items are called scope options.
- Scopes are created through the DHCP utility using the New Scope command from the Action menu, which starts the New Scope Wizard. You can also set DHCP options of default gateway, DNS servers, and WINS servers for this scope through the wizard. Myriad other options are available through a scope's properties.
- IP addresses within a scope can be reserved for specific clients, but the MAC address of that client is required to define the reservation.

OBJECTIVES ON THE JOB

Scopes or address pools are key to how DHCP operates. If there are no additional free addresses in a scope, newly booted clients are unable to communicate with the network. Scopes can simply be a block of IP addresses ready to be assigned to any client that boots, or they can be completely controlled through reservations or option classes (see Objective 2.4).

PRACTICE TEST QUESTIONS

1. **The New Scope Wizard can be used to define which of the following scope elements? (Choose all that apply.)**
    a. Default gateway
    b. All possible options
    c. Start and end IP addresses
    d. HOSTS files
    e. Active Directory host object
    f. Lease period
    g. Exclusions
2. **Which of the following statements is true? (Choose all that apply.)**
    a. Without scopes, DHCP cannot function.
    b. If a free IP address is available within a scope, it can be assigned to a requesting client.
    c. DHCP scopes are used only for Windows 2000 clients.
    d. Specific addresses within a scope can be set aside for specific clients.
3. **What is the default lease period?**
    a. Three days
    b. Six hours
    c. 24 hours
    d. Eight days
4. **Which of the following is considered a scope option? (Choose all that apply.)**
    a. WINS server addresses
    b. Subnet mask
    c. DNS server addresses
    d. Default gateway
5. **Which of the following is required to define a reservation?**
    a. System name
    b. User name
    c. MAC address
    d. Domain name
6. **Within a scope, it is possible to block specific IP addresses so they are not assigned to DHCP clients.**
    a. True
    b. False
7. **If all the addresses in a scope are leased, the DHCP server double-leases addresses so two clients can share the same configuration.**
    a. True
    b. False

OBJECTIVES

2.4 Manage DHCP scopes

SCOPE OPTIONS

UNDERSTANDING THE OBJECTIVE

Scope options can be used to define additional IP configuration settings required by unique configurations of a network, subnet, router, or client. In addition, with the use of option classes, settings can be focused on specific groups of clients that need unique configurations.

WHAT YOU REALLY NEED TO KNOW

- The most commonly used scope options are default gateway (router), domain name, DNS servers, and WINS servers.
- There are 75 available scope options on a Windows 2000 DHCP server, such as log servers, cookie servers, host name, broadcast address, static route option, **NetBIOS** scope ID, **SMTP** server, **POP3** server, and **WWW** server.
- The common scope options can be defined through the New Scope Wizard, but all other options must be manually defined after a scope is created.
- Scope options need not be applied only to the client using a scope; you can define options at four levels: server, scope, class, and reserved client. Server options are defined through the Server Options item, as are scope options. Class options are defined below. Reserved client options are defined by selecting the client reservation within the Reservations item and issuing the Configure Options command. The order of priority for options settings is: reserved client (the highest), class, scope, and server (the lowest).
- Class options (or option classes) are applied to clients that belong to a specific class of clients. These are defined on the Advanced tab of the Scope Options dialog box. There are two types of classes: vendor and user. Vendor classes are used to define options based on the operating system; user classes are custom defined. These classes can be used to create complex variances in IP configuration for each group of clients.

OBJECTIVES ON THE JOB

Scope options allow you to expand and exploit DHCP. You can apply complex and specific IP configurations to clients using scope options in conjunction with option classes. The ability to fine-tune client configurations from a single centralized DHCP server reduces administrative time by preventing manual at-the-client configuration.

PRACTICE TEST QUESTIONS

1. **HOS Corp. has a large network consisting of over 3000 clients and nearly 180 servers. All of the systems are running Windows 2000 Server or Windows 2000 Professional. Only workers in the research department need Internet access to perform daily tasks. Three DSL connections are used to establish links with the ISP, and a block of 50 IP addresses is leased from the ISP. No more than 40 researchers are connected to the LAN simultaneously due to sliding work shifts.**

   All of the client systems on the network are managed using DHCP. Those clients that connect to the Internet have all of their traffic directed to a router/firewall. All packets destined for the internal network are routed inward; all packets destined for the Internet are routed outward. Can DHCP handle the assignment of Internet access addresses to the research workers' systems, while preventing nonresearch workers' systems from using them?

   a. No, this cannot be accomplished with DHCP.
   b. Yes, an inactive scope should be defined for the research systems.
   c. Yes, an option class should be used to define unique settings for the research systems.
   d. Yes, a server option should be defined to grant Internet access to clients.

2. **HOS Corp. has decided that leasing 50 IP addresses is too expensive. Instead, it leased only three IP addresses for the DSL connections and deployed a proxy server. All internal clients use private IP addresses. Their policy about allowing only research clients to access the Internet still stands. Can DHCP be used to manage this new situation?**

   a. Yes, each research system should have a client reservation.
   b. Yes, a class option should be used to provide the IP address of the proxy server as the default gateway to only the research systems.
   c. Yes, each research system should have manually defined addresses of DNS servers located on the Internet.
   d. No, static IP addresses are required.

3. **What are the levels of options supported by Windows 2000 DHCP? (Choose all that apply.)**

   a. Kiosk
   b. Server
   c. Scope
   d. Subnet
   e. Class
   f. Domain
   g. Reservation

4. **Which option level has the highest priority?**

   a. Server
   b. Scope
   c. Class
   d. Reserved client

OBJECTIVES

2.5 Create and manage DHCP superscopes and multicast scopes

SUPERSCOPES • MULTICAST SCOPES • MADCAP

UNDERSTANDING THE OBJECTIVE

When two or more scopes are grouped together, they are collectively referred to as a superscope. Superscopes are used to expand an existing scope or to use multiple IP blocks without a router. Multicast scopes are used to define groups of systems that share a multicast address.

WHAT YOU REALLY NEED TO KNOW

- The scopes within a superscope are called child or member scopes.
- All scopes within a superscope are managed as a single entity. Thus, all IP addresses within a superscope are seen as a single pool.
- Superscopes are most often used to expand the number of IP addresses available to DHCP clients. They are also used to subnet a network without using a router and to migrate from one IP address range to another.
- Superscopes are created by issuing the New Superscope command from the Action menu when your DHCP server is selected. You can also create new scopes within a superscope.
- Multicast scopes are created using the New Multicast Scope Wizard, and do not have reservations or options. Their default lease length is 30 days.
- Multicast addresses are used to send communications to an entire group of systems instead of just a single system. This type of system is often used to distribute real-time or streaming media. Support for multicast scopes is through **MADCAP**, which is a proposed Internet standard. Multicast scopes assign Class D IP addresses (224.0.0.0 – 239.255.255.255). Class D addresses can be used privately.
- A client with a normal IP address can be assigned a multicast address as well. This allows a client to participate in normal network communications as well as multimedia broadcasts. However, the client must support MADCAP to accept transmissions.

OBJECTIVES ON THE JOB

Superscopes simplify the need to expand the number of available IP addresses required by a network. If subnets are designed with too few addresses for current growth, using superscopes avoids the need to re-subnet a network. Multicast scopes are especially useful for internal broadcasts of audio or video for training or entertainment purposes.

PRACTICE TEST QUESTIONS

1. **On The Air Corp. is testing a new in-house capability to broadcast their six pay-per-view channels to several local theaters. These theaters will be equipped with audio and video devices connected to a client computer. The client systems are all connected to On The Air's LAN via dedicated fiber-optic lines. The number of theaters involved in the testing varies each week; sometimes there are 60 theaters, sometimes only 24. The system administrators responsible for maintaining the connections between the LAN and the theater-based clients want an easy mechanism to distribute the multimedia feed. Which of the following would result in the best solution for this situation?**
   a. Static IP address assignment for each theater client
   b. A superscope for all theater clients
   c. A scope with scope options to define a DNS server
   d. Multicast scope used to define a Class D address on all theater clients
2. **Once the solution is chosen by On The Air Corp., what is the next item they must address?**
   a. Ability of fiber-optic lines to support their transmissions
   b. Client support for MADCAP
   c. Leasing requirement for Class D addresses
   d. Magnetic interference by subway trains
3. **A client system can be assigned a normal IP address and a multicast address at the same time.**
   a. True
   b. False
4. **A superscope should be used in which of the following situations? (Choose all that apply.)**
   a. When an existing scope is too small
   b. Migrating a group of clients from one subnet to another
   c. Combining multiple noncontinuous IP address ranges into a single pool
   d. When unique class options are required by various groups of clients
5. **Which of the following is true? (Choose all that apply.)**
   a. All clients in a multiscope receive the same network communications.
   b. Multiscopes assign Class D addresses.
   c. Clients can have reservations within a multiscope.
   d. The default lease period for multiscopes is eight days.
6. **Each scope within a superscope can have unique class options defined.**
   a. True
   b. False
7. **New child scopes can be added by creating new scopes within a superscope, but no other pre-existing scopes can be moved into a superscope.**
   a. True
   b. False

OBJECTIVES

2.6 Configure DHCP for DNS integration

INTEGRATE • DHCP • DNS

UNDERSTANDING THE OBJECTIVE

DHCP can integrate with Dynamic DNS. This integration provides for automated updates to DNS zones with regard to newly booted clients. Using this integration further reduces the administrative overhead involved in manually updating DNS in relation to new clients.

WHAT YOU REALLY NEED TO KNOW

- DHCP is already integrated into Dynamic DNS under Windows 2000. There are two additional requirements to make the system function: 1) both DHCP and DNS must be installed and working on the network, and 2) all DHCP clients should be configured to "Register this connection's addresses in DNS" on the DNS tab of Advanced TCP/IP Settings of a network connection object.
- Each time a client boots, it automatically registers its newly obtained IP address configuration with DNS.
- With the integration of DHCP with DNS, Microsoft has eliminated the need for WINS on Microsoft networks from an operating system standpoint.
- The announcement of IP settings from a client to the DNS server is a capability of Windows 2000 Professional and Windows 2000 Server only.

OBJECTIVES ON THE JOB

As a network grows, maintaining the DNS zone files becomes an enormous undertaking, which can be simplified by using an integrated system to perform this task automatically. The integration of DHCP-assigned IP settings with DNS zones is more a function of the TCP/IP protocol on Windows 2000 clients than the actual service integration between DHCP and DNS. In fact, newly booted clients with static IP addresses announce their settings to the DNS server if properly configured to do so. That ability is not linked to obtaining IP settings from DHCP.

PRACTICE TEST QUESTIONS

1. **POTER Inc. has a network of over 300 clients. Due to poor design planning, the network can use only 200 IP addresses from a scattering of ranges. Fortunately, only about 180 of the clients are ever booted and online at any given time. The network administrators created a superscope to combine all of the IP address ranges into a single manageable scope. Various scope options are defined for gateways, specialty servers, and DNS servers. Each client system has as its computer name the name of its primary user, with the characters "CMP" appended. A script on the Web server polls the DNS server every 15 minutes to create a list of booted computers and the user most likely logged on to each client. To ensure that the DNS server is aware of every booted system's host name and IP address, which of the following must be true?**
    a. A caching server must be deployed.
    b. A multicast scope must be defined for all clients.
    c. The Register this connection's addresses in DNS option should be enabled.
    d. A reverse lookup zone must be created.

2. **After ensuring that the selection from Question 1 is deployed, how can a system administrator verify that clients are properly listed by the DNS server?**
    a. Check the multicast usage log.
    b. View the domain's zone file contents.
    c. Examine the dns.log file.
    d. View the DHCP server performance statistics.

3. **Any computer on a Microsoft network can have its DHCP-assigned settings automatically added to DNS.**
    a. True
    b. False

4. **Both DHCP clients and clients with static IP addresses can register with DNS.**
    a. True
    b. False

5. **Where is DHCP integration with DNS primarily configured?**
    a. The DHCP server
    b. The DNS server
    c. An Active Directory domain controller
    d. A Windows 2000 client

6. **Integrating DHCP clients into DNS simplifies large network management.**
    a. True
    b. False

7. **When DNS and DHCP are interacting properly, what other Microsoft network service is no longer required by the operating system?**
    a. RAS
    b. NetBIOS
    c. WINS
    d. RIS

OBJECTIVES

2.7 Using DHCP on routed networks

DHCP RELAY AGENT

UNDERSTANDING THE OBJECTIVE

Through the use of a DHCP relay server, requests from a DHCP client can be forwarded directly to a DHCP server in a different subnet. DHCP can only be realistically deployed on routed networks with the use of the DHCP relay agent.

WHAT YOU REALLY NEED TO KNOW

- For DHCP to function properly on a routed network, you must perform one of the following three actions:
  - Deploy a DHCP server in each subnet.
  - Configure routers to pass broadcasts.
  - Deploy a DHCP relay agent in each subnet without a DHCP server.
- The DHCP relay agent intercepts broadcasts from a DHCP client and forwards them directly to a DHCP server. From that point, the DHCP server and the DHCP client can communicate through directed transmissions.
- The DHCP relay agent can be configured on each available interface to relay DHCP packets. Other settings include the number of hops before the broadcast is discarded, and the seconds-since-boot threshold.
- Once the DHCP relay agent is installed and a DHCP server is defined, it is fully functional with a four-hop count threshold and a four-second boot threshold.

OBJECTIVES ON THE JOB

DHCP functions through the use of broadcasts from clients seeking a DHCP server. Routers, by design, prevent broadcasts from spreading from one subnet to another. This effectively prevents a DHCP server in one subnet from responding to a DHCP client in a different subnet, simply because the request for configuration settings does not reach the DHCP server. You can overcome this limitation on your network by using a DHCP relay agent, which allows for a single DHCP server to support the needs of DHCP clients in different subnets. Additionally, DHCP relay agents can be used in the same subnet as a DHCP server to provide for fault tolerance. In fact, deploying several DHCP servers across your network in different subnets with a relay agent in each ensures that every client is always able to reach a DHCP server, even if one is offline.

PRACTICE TEST QUESTIONS

1. **Lindros Inc. recently expanded its network by adding 500 clients to its existing 1300 clients. To keep IP address configuration under control, the network administrator deployed a DHCP server. Upper management demanded that network overhead traffic be reduced by dividing the network into 20 subnets, separated by routers. After the cabling change, all but the clients in the same subnet as the DHCP server were able to establish communications with the rest of the network. What should be the next step in resolving this issue?**
   a. Deploy a DHCP server in each of the subnets.
   b. Define reverse lookup zones.
   c. Deploy DHCP relay agents in each of the subnets.
   d. Create multiscope zones for each subnet.
2. **After the initial step to resolve the problem, what would be another intelligent action to improve the reliability of the DHCP process?**
   a. Define secondary zones within the existing superscope.
   b. Deploy additional DHCP servers in a few different subnets.
   c. Configure zone delegation for all subnets.
   d. Broaden the IP address pool.
3. **A single DHCP server can support clients in many subnets.**
   a. True
   b. False
4. **Through what tool are DHCP relay agents created and managed?**
   a. DHCP utility
   b. Network and Dial-up Connections utility
   c. Server applet
   d. Routing and Remote Access utility
5. **What setting within a DHCP relay agent determines how long it will wait for a local DHCP server to reply to a query before forwarding it?**
   a. Boot threshold
   b. Hop count
   c. Relay DHCP packets
   d. Reservations
6. **The DHCP relay agent, even after a DHCP server IP address is provided, must be activated before it will forward client queries.**
   a. True
   b. False
7. **Which of the following is a valid method of enabling DHCP service in multiple subnets? (Choose all that apply.)**
   a. Configure routers to pass broadcasts.
   b. Define client reservations.
   c. Deploy a DHCP relay agent in each subnet without a DHCP server.
   d. Deploy a DHCP server in each subnet.

OBJECTIVES

2.8 Troubleshoot DHCP

DHCP DATABASE FILE • JETPACK

UNDERSTANDING THE OBJECTIVE

DHCP is a fairly robust service, but problems can still occur. DHCP creates a backup of its main database file automatically, and a tool is provided to repair minor corruption in the main file.

WHAT YOU REALLY NEED TO KNOW

- The DHCP database file (dhcp.mdb) is stored in the main Windows directory in the \system32\dhcp folder.
- The DHCP database file is automatically backed up in the \system32\dhcp\backup\jet\new folder.
- The DHCP server performs a consistency check on its database when it first launches after bootup and at regular intervals. It attempts to correct any irregularities using data from the main and backup files.
- If a serious corruption of the database occurs, an error message is written to the System Log accessed through Event Viewer. Corruption errors can often be corrected using the JETPACK utility from the Windows 2000 Server distribution CD.
- Additionally, the JETPACK utility should be used regularly (once a month or once a quarter) on large DHCP databases (e.g., with 2000 clients or more). This checks the database file for errors and compacts the file to run more efficiently.
- If JETPACK fails to restore the main database file, you can perform a manual restore of the file from the backup copy.

OBJECTIVES ON THE JOB

The DHCP database file can become corrupt for a variety of reasons, such as when it grows too large for the hard drive partition on which it lives. DHCP troubleshooting typically starts with inspecting the network for communication difficulties, followed by verification of scope properties. After those avenues are exhausted, you can attempt a corruption repair or backup restoration. Before using the JETPACK utility, it is a good idea to manually back up the main DHCP database file.

PRACTICE TEST QUESTIONS

1. **The backup of the main DHCP database file is stored where?**
   a. \system32\dhcp\backup\jet\new folder
   b. \Program Files\dhcp
   c. \system32\dhcp folder
   d. in each user's home directory
2. **Which tool can be used to repair a corrupted database file?**
   a. System applet
   b. JETPACK
   c. Disk Management
   d. Convert
3. **DHCP is fairly robust, maintains a backup of its main database file, and attempts to repair minor problems on the fly.**
   a. True
   b. False
4. **Which of the following is a valid step when attempting to repair a corrupted DHCP database file? (Choose all that apply.)**
   a. Running JETPACK
   b. Starting the DHCP service
   c. Defining scope options
   d. Changing to the \system32\dhcp\backup\jet\new folder
5. **You are the network administrator for a medium-sized network. Each client is assigned its IP configuration upon bootup by a single DHCP server. This morning, you discovered that the DHCP server is not responding to client requests for new leases. You attempt to troubleshoot the problem by checking network connections, rebooting the server hosting DHCP, and verifying scope property settings. What is the next best course of action?**
   a. Open the dhcp.mdb file in a text editor.
   b. View the contents of the zone file.
   c. Remove DNS.
   d. View the System Log through Event Viewer.
6. **After the course of action in Question 5 has been executed, you discover that your database is corrupted. After executing the JETPACK tool against the main database file, the system is still not functioning. At this point, what is your next best option?**
   a. Remove and then reinstall DHCP.
   b. Delete all database files and re-create all scopes.
   c. Restore the DHCP database file from backup.
   d. Reconfigure clients with static IP addresses.
7. **A DHCP server regularly verifies that its working database file is free from errors.**
   a. True
   b. False

OBJECTIVES

2.9 Manage and monitor DHCP

DHCP • SYSTEM MONITOR • SYSTEM LOG • SCOPE

UNDERSTANDING THE OBJECTIVE

The operation of DHCP is invisible to the user. In fact, unless a problem occurs, there is little obvious activity related to DHCP. Monitoring DHCP can be performed through System Monitor or through logging.

WHAT YOU REALLY NEED TO KNOW

- System Monitor can view the performance metrics related to DHCP by watching the counters from the DHCP server object.
- The DHCP server automatically logs start-up, shutdown, and error reports related to the DHCP service to the System Log.
- The DHCP server also records its own internal activities in a log file by default. The log file is stored in the \system32\dhcp folder in a file named dhcpsrvlog.xxx (where xxx are the first three letters of the day of the week). This log is a text file, which can be viewed through any text editor. Only the last seven days of log data are retained.
- This internal logging can be disabled.
- You can see current statistics on a scope-by-scope basis by issuing the Display Statistics command from the Action menu when a scope is selected. Data displayed includes the total number of IP addresses in the scope, the number leased, and the number available.
- If you must delete a scope from a DHCP server or completely remove DHCP from a Windows 2000 Server system, ensure that all clients have a method of obtaining their configurations. The following are some tips to make the transition smoother:
  - Set a short lease duration on the scope to be removed. The lease expires shortly after the scope is removed, and an alternate scope should be available to meet clients' future needs.
  - Verify, after you have removed the old scope, that clients properly obtained a new lease from the new scope. You can force this with the commands ipconfig /release and then ipconfig /renew.
  - Keep track of reservations. If a client needs a reserved address, be sure to create a reservation for it in the new scope.
  - Verify that the new scope or new DHCP server has enough free IP addresses to support the clients added to it from the old scope/server.

OBJECTIVES ON THE JOB

DHCP management lies in creating and manipulating scopes and options, configuring clients, and checking the database for corruption. Otherwise, DHCP is self-sufficient. Fortunately, DHCP records events and problems to log files, so you can quickly detect a problem.

PRACTICE TEST QUESTIONS

1. **Through what method or mechanism can you obtain information about the activity of a DHCP server? (Choose all that apply.)**
   a. Event Viewer
   b. System applet
   c. System Monitor
   d. Log file
2. **Which of the following is an example of the name of the DHCP log file?**
   a. dhcp.log
   b. dhcpsvrlog.mon
   c. dhcplog.txt
   d. dhcp.mdb
3. **Logging is enabled by default on a DHCP server.**
   a. True
   b. False
4. **What type of event does a DHCP server record in the System Log? (Choose all that apply.)**
   a. Service start
   b. Error
   c. Service shutdown
   d. Client lease assignment
5. **Which of the following is a useful step in migrating a set of clients from an old scope to a new scope? (Choose all that apply.)**
   a. Set a short lease duration on the old scope.
   b. Shut down all clients before removing the old scope.
   c. Make sure the new scope has enough available IP addresses for the newly added systems.
   d. Re-create the reservations needed.
   e. Define a static IP address temporarily while the DHCP server configuration changes are taking place.
   f. Force configuration renewal after removing the old scope.
   g. Place the old scope in a superscope along with the new scope.
6. **Counters from which object should be used within System Monitor to view DHCP performance?**
   a. DHCP
   b. DHCP Server
   c. DHCP Service
   d. DHCP Clients
7. **The DHCP utility offers a quick look at current lease statistics.**
   a. True
   b. False

Section 3

Configuring, Managing, Monitoring, and Troubleshooting Remote Access in a Windows 2000 Network Infrastructure

OBJECTIVES

3.1 Configure and troubleshoot remote access

REMOTE ACCESS LINKS • PPP

UNDERSTANDING THE OBJECTIVE

Remote access is the ability to connect to or answer connections from remote systems. This means a local system can establish a network link over a phone line or other medium with a different server or network. Remote access is key to sharing resources between otherwise disconnected networks.

WHAT YOU REALLY NEED TO KNOW

- The Routing and Remote Access utility is a fully integrated part of Windows 2000. It supports a wide range of routing capabilities, proxying, and inbound and outbound connections.
- All remote access links are full-service network links. A client connected over a remote access link can perform the same functions as a client connected directly to the LAN with a cable; the only difference is speed.
- Windows 2000, through Routing and Remote Access, boasts the following features:
  - **VPN** connection using **PPTP** or **L2TP**
  - **NAT**
  - **ICS**
  - **RADIUS**
  - Multilink PPP
  - Static/dynamic/demand-dial routing
  - Multiprotocol routing (IP, **IPX**, AppleTalk)
  - Callback and caller ID security
  - Improved authentication and encryption protocols
  - Security control through group policy and remote access protocols
- Remote access links are usually **PPP**, but **SLIP** is still supported for connecting to legacy systems. Thus, Windows 2000 can connect with any Microsoft operating system and most other operating systems.
- Routing and Remote Access can be managed through a GUI or the Net Shell (netsh) command.

OBJECTIVES ON THE JOB

Routing and Remote Access enables a stand-alone system or a network of any size to reach out and communicate with other systems and networks. With native routing capabilities, Windows 2000 Server can act as a multihomed router to direct traffic or simply provide services on two different subnets. With native remote access capabilities, Windows 2000 can accept inbound connections from remote clients, offer Internet access to network clients, establish high-speed communication links with distant networks, and even create secure network connections over the Internet for virtual private networking.

PRACTICE TEST QUESTIONS

1. **Which of the following is true? (Choose all that apply.)**
   a. Routing and Remote Access is a service that must be installed in Windows 2000.
   b. All remote access links are full-service network links.
   c. Routing can only be managed through a command line.
   d. Both SLIP and PPP can be used to establish connections to other systems.
2. **Routing and Remote Access can be managed from a GUI and a command-line interface.**
   a. True
   b. False
3. **Routing and Remote Access provides what type of functionality for Windows 2000 networks? (Choose all that apply.)**
   a. Network links to remote systems
   b. Proxied access to the Internet
   c. Firewall protection
   d. Answering inbound connection attempts
4. **Routing and Remote Access enables a stand-alone system or a network of any size to communicate with other systems and networks.**
   a. True
   b. False
5. **With native remote access capabilities, Windows 2000 can ______. (Choose all that apply.)**
   a. accept inbound connections from remote clients
   b. offer Internet access to network clients
   c. establish high-speed communication links with distant networks
   d. create secure network connections over the Internet for virtual private networking

OBJECTIVES

3.2 Configure inbound remote access connections

INBOUND AND OUTBOUND CONNECTIONS • PPP

UNDERSTANDING THE OBJECTIVE

A popular feature of remote access is to allow remote clients to connect to your LAN. Windows 2000 can accept only PPP inbound connections.

WHAT YOU REALLY NEED TO KNOW

- ◆ You create and configure inbound and outbound connections through the Network and Dial-up Connections utility on Windows 2000 Professional and nondomain controller Windows 2000 servers. On domain controllers, you manage them through the Routing and Remote Access utility.
- ◆ Windows 2000 Server can support up to 256 inbound connections, while Windows 2000 Professional can support only one.
- ◆ From the Network and Dial-up Connections utility, create inbound connections through the Network Connection Wizard's Accept incoming connections option. The creation process prompts for the following: which devices can accept inbound connections, whether to allow VPNs over this connection object, whether to grant users access (and configure per-user callback restrictions), and which networking components to access through this connection object.
- ◆ From the Routing and Remote Access utility, you allow inbound connections by issuing the Configure and Enable Routing and Remote Access command and selecting the Remote Access server options. Once the service starts, the system answers inbound connections.
- ◆ Once the inbound connection object is created, its icon appears in the Network and Dial-up Connections utility.
- ◆ The device used by an inbound connection cannot be used by any other inbound connection. However, the device can be used by outbound connection objects.
- ◆ Once an inbound connection object has been created, it is active. It answers the next inbound call.

OBJECTIVES ON THE JOB

In order to handle more than four inbound connections, you must deploy a multiport modem device or use VPN connections over a high-speed Internet link. Generally, you should not configure inbound connections on a domain controller due to the additional overhead and complexity. While Windows 2000 is limited to accepting PPP connections, this does not limit the **LAN** protocol or client operating system used over that connection. In fact, any of the supported protocols (TCP/IP, **NWLink**, and **NetBEUI**) can be used over the PPP link and any client-supported PPP can establish a connection (assuming a valid user name and password are provided).

PRACTICE TEST QUESTIONS

1. **How many inbound connections are supported by Windows 2000 Server?**
    a. one
    b. eight
    c. 128
    d. 256
2. **What type of connection is supported for inbound links to Windows 2000?**
    a. SLIP
    b. RPC
    c. PPP
    d. ROTFL
3. **Windows 2000 Professional is limited to a single inbound connection.**
    a. True
    b. False
4. **What tool can be used to create inbound connection objects? (Choose all that apply.)**
    a. Network and Dial-up Connections
    b. Phone and Modem Options
    c. Internet Options
    d. Routing and Remote Access
5. **The Network Connection Wizard, when creating an inbound connection object, prompts for which of the following items? (Choose all that apply.)**
    a. Grant users access permissions
    b. Time period when remote access is allowed
    c. Devices that can accept inbound connections
    d. Group policy selection
    e. Whether to allow VPNs
    f. Networking components to be accessed through this connection object
    g. Bandwidth throttle settings
6. **Which of the following statements is true? (Choose all that apply.)**
    a. A single modem device can be used by multiple inbound connection objects.
    b. Once an inbound connection object is created, it automatically answers the next dial-in attempt.
    c. Any Windows 2000-supported LAN protocol can be used over an inbound connection.
    d. VPN links cannot be established over inbound connections.
    e. Any client supporting PPP can connect to a Windows 2000 system.
7. **A modem device configured for use by an outbound connection cannot be configured for use by an inbound connection.**
    a. True
    b. False

OBJECTIVES

3.3 Create a remote access policy

REMOTE ACCESS POLICY

UNDERSTANDING THE OBJECTIVE

Remote access policies are used to exert control over a user or group in regard to dial-in and dial-out privileges. Remote access policies are similar to group policies.

WHAT YOU REALLY NEED TO KNOW

- Remote access policies are defined through the Routing and Remote Access utility.
- The default remote access policy is named "Allow access if dial-in permission is enabled." This policy contains a single condition that allows inbound connections 24 hours a day, 7 days a week.
- New remote access policies can be defined by issuing the New, Remote Access Policy command from the Action menu when the Remote Access Policies folder is selected. After providing a name for the policy, you can define one or more conditions required by this policy and grant or deny remote access based on matching condition criteria.
- Multiple policies can be defined to fine-tune control over your remote access system. Additionally, remote access policies have a priority order so the highest priority policy has the most influence. However, settings on the Dial-in tab of a user account's properties override any remote access policies.
- Remote access policies apply only when native mode is used. Mixed mode does not support remote access policies.
- Some of the conditions available through a remote policy include caller ID, time period, protocol used, tunneling protocol used, and service requested.
- Remote access policies can be applied to specific groups of users by selecting the Windows groups condition.

OBJECTIVES ON THE JOB

Remote access policies can be created to apply to all dial-in clients or to specific groups only. You perform this simply by adding or omitting the Windows groups condition in the policy itself. Thus, you should plan your policies before creating them. Also, because each policy defines a set of conditions and whether to grant or deny access based on those conditions, you should consider the logic of your selections. Make sure the results you want are what you get; test your policies before deploying them in a production environment.

PRACTICE TEST QUESTIONS

1. **BLOP Corp. has a large number of telecommuters, all of whom are scheduled to work a shift from 9 p.m. to 5 a.m. However, records show they have been connecting to the LAN at all hours of the day. While this grants them flexibility in accomplishing their work tasks, the LAN cannot support the additional workload. Thus, management decreed that all telecommuters be restricted to accessing the network between 8 p.m. and 6 a.m. During all other hours, too many direct-connect clients consume the bandwidth of the network. The company does not wish to spend additional funds on increasing the capacity of the network; rather, they wish to control user connections in order to manage the network load. In addition to the telecommuting rule, management also decreed that all direct-connect users must log off before 8 p.m. and cannot log on until 6 a.m. Which of the following actions should you take to impose management's new rules through Windows 2000?**
   a. Create a group policy that limits remote access connections.
   b. Create a remote access policy that limits connections to 8 p.m. to 6 a.m.
   c. Configure connection timeouts for all users.
   d. Disable dial-In connections for all users who do not telecommute.
2. **After you implement your solution, a manager discovers that, when she attempted to log on to the LAN from her home system at 10:30 p.m. one evening, she was not able to establish a connection. What is the best course of action to grant this manager (and others) exclusion from the remote access restriction?**
   a. Place all telecommuter user accounts in a group named RASUSERS, and add a Windows group condition to the remote access policy.
   b. Manually enable Allow access on the Dial-in tab of each user account as needed.
   c. Reconfigure each home workstation to connect using SLIP.
   d. None of the above
3. **Without the Windows groups condition, remote access policies apply to all users.**
   a. True
   b. False
4. **Which of the following statements is true? (Choose all that apply.)**
   a. Remote access policies only apply when native mode is used.
   b. The default remote access policy contains a single condition that allows inbound connections 24 hours a day, 7 days a week.
   c. Mixed mode does not support remote access policies.
   d. Remote access policies are defined through the Network and Dial-up Connections utility.
   e. Settings on the Dial-in tab of a user account's properties override any remote access policies.

OBJECTIVES

3.4 Configure a remote access profile

REMOTE ACCESS PROFILE • DIAL-IN

UNDERSTANDING THE OBJECTIVE

A remote access profile is a set of conditions that are applied to a connection after it is authorized to occur (that is, it has passed the policy restrictions). Profiles are defined on a per-policy level: Each policy has its own profile.

WHAT YOU REALLY NEED TO KNOW

- You define remote access profiles within a remote access policy. They apply only to those users who match the criteria of that remote access profile.
- A remote access profile can be created at the same time the policy is created, or it can be defined after a remote access policy is created.
- You create and manage remote access profiles by clicking the Edit Profile button on the last page of the Remote Access Policy Creation Wizard or on the Settings tab of a remote access profile's properties dialog box.
- The Edit Dial-in Profile dialog box has six tabs of configuration options:
  - Dial-in Constraints: set idle disconnect, maximum session length, restrict access times/days, dial-in number restriction, dial-in media type restriction
  - IP: set IP address assignment to server supplies, client request, or server defines; also define to client and from client IP packet filters
  - Multilink: set to server defined, disable, or allow with maximum ports; set bandwidth allocation protocol in % capacity and minutes to reduce multilink connection by one line
  - Authentication: set allowed authentication protocols for link—extensible authentication protocol (MD 5-challenge, smart card-certificate), **MS-CHAP**, MS-CHAP v2, **CHAP**, **PAP/SPAP**, none
  - Encryption: set allowed encryption levels—none, basic, strong
  - Advanced: used to define RADIUS attributes

OBJECTIVES ON THE JOB

Through clever use of profiles in conjunction with policies, you can effectively control the dial-in environment of all remote users. Keep in mind that policies can be configured to apply to specific groups of users; thus, a profile can be fine-tuned to properly grant or restrict remote access capabilities for that group.

PRACTICE TEST QUESTIONS

1. **SKYBAT Inc. has a large number of telecommuting employees. Many of them are researchers, while a few are in the finance department. There have been several corporate espionage attempts over the last few years, against which you must protect the network. The research team connecting to the LAN remotely does not manage sensitive material, but users in the finance department do. What can you do to protect the integrity of the data handled by the remote finance users specifically without altering any other user connections? (Choose all that apply.)**
    a. Create a remote access policy that applies only to the finance users.
    b. Define a group policy that requires strong encryption and authentication.
    c. Define a remote access profile that only allows strong encryption and MS-CHAP v2 authentication.
    d. Deploy DLS connections for remote users.
    e. Use cable modems for all remote users and establish a VPN.
2. **After implementing your choices, you discover that many connections remain open for extended periods of time with no activity. You realize this may result in a security breach and, at the least, is a waste of resources. What can you do to correct this issue?**
    a. Restrict access times and days on the remote access profile.
    b. Define an idle disconnect time on the remote access profile.
    c. Configure BAP to disconnect when 50% of capacity is used for more than two minutes on the remote access profile.
    d. Define a maximum session limit on the remote access profile.
3. **Remote access profiles are defined within a remote access policy and apply only to users who match the criteria of that remote access profile.**
    a. True
    b. False
4. **Which of the following statements is true? (Choose all that apply.)**
    a. A remote access profile can be created at the same time the policy is created, or it can be defined after a remote access policy is created.
    b. Each remote access profile is attached to one or more remote access policies.
    c. Remote access profiles are defined separately from remote access policies and must be manually attached to remote access policies to function.
    d. Remote access can be configured to apply a remote access profile to a specific user.
5. **Which of the following is a possible or valid setting within a remote access profile? (Choose all that apply.)**
    a. Restrict the minimum session time in minutes.
    b. Set callback security.
    c. Define a percentage of bandwidth usage to a length of time to initiate a one-line reduction in a multilink connection.
    d. Allow the client to request an IP address.
    e. Allow remote clients to connect with no authentication.

OBJECTIVES

3.5 Configure a virtual private network (VPN)

VPN • PPTP • L2TP • IPSEC

UNDERSTANDING THE OBJECTIVE

VPNs are a networking technology solution that enables secure private network links to be created over an insecure public network, such as the Internet. Windows 2000 natively supports VPN connections.

WHAT YOU REALLY NEED TO KNOW

- Windows 2000 VPN links use one of two protocols: PPTP or L2TP (**IPSec**). L2TP is standards-based, while PPTP is proprietary to Microsoft. L2TP is supported by many platforms; PPTP is supported only by Windows operating systems and Linux.
- Routing and Remote Access automatically supports VPN links.
- On systems not using Routing and Remote Access, you enable or disable VPN support for any inbound connection object via a check box on its General Properties tab.
- VPN link ports are configured within the Ports folder of the Routing and Remote Access utility. From the Ports' properties dialog box, you can access the configuration dialog for the five PPTP and five L2TP ports made available by default.
- To use only one VPN protocol and not the other, set the number of ports on one of the protocols to zero. (The VPN protocol cannot be deleted or removed from the system.)
- On the client, a VPN connection object must be created. After the object is created, you can configure it through its properties. The object is set, by default, to detect the VPN server type (PPTP or L2TP) automatically. The object can also be configured to dial an Internet connection before attempting the VPN link.
- L2TP requires that IPSec policies be in place. In most cases, you can define this through the group policy for the domain. Fortunately, a reasonable set of policies is defined by default.

OBJECTIVES ON THE JOB

VPN links are established within a pre-existing Internet (or other public network) link. To accept VPN connections from remote clients, the Routing and Remote Access server must have an open, dedicated Internet connection, and the client must have an open Internet connection. A VPN server's Internet connection is used exclusively for VPN links. If a normal Internet connection is required, a second distinct connection must be deployed.

PRACTICE TEST QUESTIONS

1. **JYS Corp. sells printing equipment to packaging plants. It has a central office in New York. It also has 15 remote support technicians who travel throughout the U.S. to maintain equipment at customer locations. Each technician must regularly connect to the central office LAN to exchange data, reports, manuals, software updates, and so on. Until recently, the remote technicians made long-distance calls to the central office LAN, and each call typically lasted 45 minutes or more. This resulted in an unbudgeted phone expense that management has demanded be reduced, if not removed. What is your best choice from the following options? (Choose all that apply.)**
   a. Provide each remote technician with an ISP account with local dial-up access in each major city, and configure the central office LAN to accept VPN links.
   b. Employ overnight delivery of CD-Rs between remote technicians and the central office LAN.
   c. Set a remote access profile to restrict connections to 15 minutes.
   d. Only allow a single remote user to connect at a time.
2. **After implementing your solution, management asks you to prevent PPTP VPN links, because they recently read a newspaper article about how a PPTP link over the Internet might be susceptible to a blocking attack by hackers. How do you implement this?**
   a. Uninstall the PPTP protocol.
   b. Set the L2TP to top-priority use in the Routing and Remote Access utility.
   c. Set encryption to support only IPSec.
   d. Set the maximum number of ports on PPTP to zero.
3. **VPN links are supported automatically within Routing and Remote Access.**
   a. True
   b. False
4. **Which of the following statements is true? (Choose all that apply.)**
   a. On nondomain controllers, VPN support is controlled through a check box.
   b. An Internet connection is required by all VPN links.
   c. Non-Windows clients can establish a VPN link with Windows 2000.
   d. Windows 2000 VPN client connection objects are set, by default, to detect the VPN server connection type automatically.
   e. A client connection object can predial an Internet connection before attempting the VPN link.
5. **Both L2TP and PPTP require additional security configurations before VPN links using them can be established.**
   a. True
   b. False

OBJECTIVES

3.6 Configure multilink connections

MULTILINK • BAP

UNDERSTANDING THE OBJECTIVE

Multilink is the ability to aggregate two or more remote access links into a single communications pipeline. Multilink is managed by BAP.

WHAT YOU REALLY NEED TO KNOW

- Multilink is initiated by the client and must be supported by the answering remote access server.
- Multilink allows multiple communication devices on a single system to be aggregated. Multilink cannot aggregate communication devices on different systems.
- Multilink cannot be used with callback security.
- Multilink is enabled on a Windows 2000 remote access server simply by setting two or more devices to answer incoming connections and marking the Enable Multilink or Multilink Connections check box.
- Unique multilink settings can be defined through a remote access profile. On the Multilink tab, multilink can be disabled or set to a maximum number of ports per user. You can also define **BAP** to reduce the multilink connection by one line if bandwidth use remains below a specified percentage for a specified length of time (only applicable when the client is configured to dial devices as needed).
- Use BAP to add or remove links based on bandwidth consumption. BAP does not disconnect the last line of a connection.
- On the Options tab of a connection object, multilink can be defined to dial all devices, to dial only the first device, or to dial devices as needed. The latter selection allows for settings to define when to add or remove links, based on bandwidth usage during a time period.

OBJECTIVES ON THE JOB

Through the use of multilink, the bandwidth of a single system can be increased simply by adding more connections of the same type, rather than upgrading to a faster connection technology. In most cases, adding a second or third line of the same technology is less expensive than migrating to a faster technology.

PRACTICE TEST QUESTIONS

1. **All remote users at Way Out Inc. dial in to the central LAN over conventional phone lines. However, many use multiple connections at one time to improve their overall bandwidth. The central LAN has 128 inbound phone lines, and there are 84 remote employees. In most cases, only 30 or so employees are simultaneously connected. In order to guarantee that there are available lines to up to 35 employees, what limitation should be enforced?**
    a. Set a remote access profile to disable multilink.
    b. Set a remote access profile to allow multilink of up to three ports.
    c. Set BAP to drop lines with 40% capacity for five minutes.
    d. Configure clients to dial all devices.
2. **Management decided to transform the 128 phone lines from normal lines to toll lines. A toll line incurs a charge only when in use. They were able to strike a contract with the phone company to limit the toll charges incurred, up to the amount that would be charged if the lines were normal lines. Management requested that measures be put in place that cause the least number of phone lines to be used by remote employees, in order to keep expenses to a minimum. Which of the following changes should be made to implement this policy? (Choose all that apply.)**
    a. Set a remote access profile to use BAP at 50% for two minutes.
    b. Set clients to dial as needed.
    c. Set clients to dial all devices.
    d. Set a remote access profile to allow multilink of up to four ports.
3. **Multilink can be used with callback security.**
    a. True
    b. False
4. **Which of the following statements is true? (Choose all that apply.)**
    a. Multilink can aggregate communication devices on different systems.
    b. Multilink allows multiple communication devices on a single system to be aggregated.
    c. Multilink must be supported and enabled on both the client and server to function.
    d. A multilink client can connect to a server on which multilink is not enabled.
    e. BAP is used to add or remove links based on bandwidth consumption.
    f. BAP disconnects the last line of a connection when its usage falls below the specified limit.
    g. BAP, on the client, can be configured to add lines as well as remove them.

OBJECTIVES

3.7 Configure Routing and Remote Access for DHCP integration

ROUTING AND REMOTE ACCESS • DHCP • DHCP RELAY AGENT

UNDERSTANDING THE OBJECTIVE

Remote access clients can obtain their IP configuration from DHCP. DHCP is easily integrated with remote access to provide a seamless connection solution.

WHAT YOU REALLY NEED TO KNOW

- Remote access clients can obtain their IP address configuration in several ways, including static configuration on the client, from a DHCP server on the remote access network (client is configured to obtain an IP address automatically), or from the remote access server's pool of static addresses (client is configured to obtain an IP address automatically).
- When Routing and Remote Access is configured to use DHCP, it requests a block of IP addresses from the DHCP server on the network. The first IP address in this block is assigned to the **RAS** interface (to be used by the remote client as its gateway address); the others are assigned to remote clients as needed. When all available addresses are assigned, another block of addresses is requested.
- The size of the block of addresses is 10 by default; this value can be altered through the Registry value of InitialAddressPoolSize.
- If DHCP is not available on the network or using it is not desired, the remote access server can be configured to assign addresses to remote clients from a static address pool.
- The DHCP configuration is defined for remote access on the IP tab of a remote access server's properties dialog box through the Routing and Remote Access utility.
- If a DHCP server is not present on the local subnet, a DHCP relay agent must be deployed to allow the remote access server to communicate with the DHCP server. The remote access server interacts with the DHCP server in the same manner as a typical DHCP client: It requests a block of IP addresses instead of a single IP address.

OBJECTIVES ON THE JOB

Microsoft recommends using DHCP instead of a static address pool for assigning remote clients their IP configurations. A remote access server is the system that manages and is responsible for the leases from the DHCP server, not the remote client. When a remote client releases an IP address, the address is returned to the remote access server, not the DHCP server, where it is assigned to the next remote client. All IP addresses leased to the remote access server are released when that service is stopped or the system is shut down. The addresses assigned to the remote access server cannot be released manually—the ipconfig /release command does not function.

PRACTICE TEST QUESTIONS

1. **LOZR Corp. has a client base of more than 400. Their primary network-related work tasks take place within an in-house–developed database interface that requires all clients to have an IP address. The program allows a maximum of 100 users to connect to it simultaneously. Fortunately, the workers operate in shifts and most connect from remote locations. There are four seven-hour shifts every day with 100 clients in each shift. Each shift overlaps the preceding and following shift by one hour. In most cases, only about 50 users are online simultaneously during a shift and only about 80 during overlaps. Which of the following is the best action to take in this situation?**
   a. Create multiple subnets with 16 clients in each subnet, and then create DHCP pools for each subnet. Define remote access profiles to assign each client to the appropriate pool.
   b. Assign static IP addresses to all clients.
   c. Configure remote access to assign IP addresses to remote access clients from a static address pool.
   d. Configure remote access to assign IP addresses to remote clients from DHCP.
2. **After deploying your solution, network tests indicate that you need to move your DHCP server from the subnet where the remote access server resides to a new and currently unpopulated subnet. Which of the following must also be performed to ensure continued operation of all capabilities?**
   a. Define the DHCP server's IP address in a remote access profile.
   b. Deploy a DHCP relay agent in each subnet without a DHCP server.
   c. Define the DHCP server's IP address on each remote client.
   d. No other actions are required.
3. **The permanent and default size of the block of addresses requested by a DHCP integrated remote access server is 10.**
   a. True
   b. False
4. **You need to test your network's DHCP configuration. Your network boasts a remote access server integrated with DHCP. You already issued the ipconfig/release command on each local system. Which of the following is a valid method for canceling the leases managed by the remote access server? (Choose all that apply.)**
   a. Issue the ipconfig /release command on each system.
   b. Disconnect the network cable to the remote access server.
   c. Stop the remote access service.
   d. Reboot the remote access system.
5. **A remote access server can assign IP addresses to clients without the use of a DHCP server.**
   a. True
   b. False

OBJECTIVES

3.8 Manage and monitor remote access

REMOTE ACCESS • PPP.LOG • LASLOG.LOG • INTERNET MIB II

UNDERSTANDING THE OBJECTIVE

Remote access is an integrated part of Windows 2000; thus, management and monitoring tools used in other areas of the network operating system can be used for remote access. You can easily monitor the activity of remote access using tools native to Windows 2000.

WHAT YOU REALLY NEED TO KNOW

- In System Monitor, you can view the performance metrics related to remote access by watching the counters from the RAS Port (to examine a single port) and RAS Total (to examine remote access as a whole) objects.
- Event details specific to remote access can be recorded in the System Log viewed through Event Viewer.
- PPP logging can be enabled on the Event Logging tab. The PPP.LOG file is recorded in the \tracing folder of the main Windows directory. The Routing and Remote Access Service must be restarted for this change to take effect.
- Details about authentication and accounting can be recorded in the \system32\LogFiles folder by configuring the log file within the Remote Access Logging section of the Routing and Remote Access utility. This file is named LASLOG.LOG and is stored in either an **IAS** (comma-delimited by default) or a database-compatible file (ODBC-compliant) format.
- Network Monitor can be used to capture traffic related to remote access, primarily in regard to PPP packets. Network Monitor cannot extract the contents of remote access communications, but it can be useful in determining the IP addresses of sender and receiver, the application and protocol types in use, and whether data is being encrypted or compressed (identified by a value of 0x3D for a packet's protocol ID).
- Remote access is compatible with **SNMP**'s Internet MIB II. This allows you to use a third-party SNMP monitoring tool to oversee the operation of Windows 2000 remote access.
- Windows 2000 remote access is compatible with many third-party monitoring tools, which comply with Microsoft **APIs**.
- The Routing and Remote Access utility offers some status and monitoring information. Selecting the Server Status element displays status statistics for the server as a whole. The Remote Access Clients element displays status statistics for each connected client.

OBJECTIVES ON THE JOB

Managing and monitoring remote access is simply the act of ensuring that each aspect of the connection, from establishment to disconnection, functions properly. The native tools of Windows 2000 provide you ample resources to execute management and monitoring.

PRACTICE TEST QUESTIONS

1. **LOOSST Inc. uses remote connections to allow traveling sales personnel to connect to the central LAN to download new pricing sheets and other product-specific information. These remote clients dial up a local ISP, then establish a VPN connection with the LAN. FTP is used to exchange sensitive documentation. The central LAN has two permanent connections to the Internet over ISDN lines. One is used exclusively for VPN links; the other is for two-way Internet traffic. Through a poor configuration setting, remote sales personnel can establish links with the central LAN without a secure link. You must track down which remote clients are failing to establish a secure VPN link before connecting to the central LAN's FTP server. Which of the following results in the fastest determination?**
   a. View the System Log through Event Viewer.
   b. Examine the LASLOG.LOG file.
   c. Use System Monitor to view bandwidth consumption.
   d. Create a capture trigger based on searching for the PPP packet's protocol ID for 0x3D.
2. **After implementing your choice, you find and correct all clients. Now, you wish to record each time an error occurs during an attempt to establish a VPN link. Which of the following actions offers the information you desire?**
   a. Use Network Monitor to view all PPP traffic.
   b. Set System Monitor to record a log of all RAS counters.
   c. Set the Event Logging tab to log errors and warnings.
   d. Disable the PPP log.
3. **The RAS Port object in System Monitor is used to view the activity of the entire remote access server at once.**
   a. True
   b. False
4. **Which of the following statements is true? (Choose all that apply.)**
   a. The System Log records events directly from the remote access server.
   b. The default file format of the LASLOG.LOG file is ODBC-compliant.
   c. Remote access is compatible with SNMP's Internet MIB II.
   d. Network Monitor can extract the contents of remote access communications.
   e. Routing and Remote Access Service must be restarted for changes to the PPP.LOG file to take effect.
5. **Which of the following settings for the Event Logging tab results in the most available system resources to handle actual remote access clients?**
   a. Log errors only
   b. Log errors and warnings
   c. Log the maximum amount of information

OBJECTIVES

3.9 Configure remote access security

REMOTE ACCESS • RADIUS • PACKET FILTERING • CALLBACK SECURITY

UNDERSTANDING THE OBJECTIVE

Security involves logon protection, data protection, and other connection and communication measures. Authentication protocols and encryption protocols are discussed in later objectives.

WHAT YOU REALLY NEED TO KNOW

- You can set the authentication provider and accounting provider in the Security tab of the remote access server's properties dialog box. There are two selections for authentication provider: Windows Authentication (the default) and RADIUS Authentication. The default setting uses the native security structure to approve remote client access. The RADIUS setting uses unique user credentials to approve remote client access.
- RADIUS servers can be defined for use by remote access. You must provide a server name, shared secret, timeout, initial score, and port. A RADIUS server can be a third-party solution or Windows 2000 Server running IAS.
- Packet filtering can be used to control traffic over remote access connections. Packet filtering can be enabled and configured on the remote access server, on the remote access adapter, or through remote access profiles.
- Callback security is defined on a per-user basis on the Dial-in tab of a user's properties. It can be set to return a connection to a predefined number or to a user-provided number. Only a predefined number offers security. Callback cannot be used for VPN or multilink connections.
- With specialized equipment, caller ID verification can be used to allow or prevent an inbound connection. Caller ID is defined on a per-user basis on the Dial-in tab of a user's properties.
- Remote access account lockout can be enabled to lock out user accounts over remote access connections (not associated with the lockout feature for local logons). This must be set through the Registry by defining values for MaxDenials and ResetTime(Mins). See the Resource Kit for details.

OBJECTIVES ON THE JOB

Consider topologies when designing and maintaining networks, because they influence performance, expense, ease of use, and troubleshooting. Network topologies affect the way computer rooms and work areas are cabled, the type of cabling and connectors used, and the type of NICs, hubs, routers, and other devices used.

PRACTICE TEST QUESTIONS

1. **KLOK Corp. supports a large number of telecommuting employees, most of whom connect over ISDN lines. The office LAN offers Internet access to its clients. Performance reports for the remote access server show that 95% of its activity is consumed by processing Web traffic for the telecommuters. Management decided that telecommuters don't need Web access to accomplish their work tasks. However, you also realize that most of the managers and executives connect remotely while on the road or at home, and they would not want the Web ban on their restrictions. Which of the following is the best choice to implement this restriction?**
   a. Define a restriction on the remote access server through the Advanced TCP/IP Properties, Options tab, Filtering option.
   b. Define a restriction through remote access profiles (within a policy) on the IP tab by defining to and from client filters.
   c. Define a restriction on the remote access adapter through the Routing and Remote Access, IP Routing, General option, open the properties dialog box for a listed interface, and then define input or output filters with manually defined exceptions.
   d. Remove Internet access for the entire network.
2. **You asked one of your system administrator interns to implement the new restriction. However, you discovered that no remote access users can access Web resources. Which of the following is a valid action to take to track down the problem? (Choose all that apply.)**
   a. Make sure the remote access policy is applied to only the telecommuting group and not to managers or executives.
   b. Make sure the managers and executives have dial-in privilege.
   c. Disable caller ID verify.
   d. Verify that filtering was not enabled on the adapter or protocol.
3. **Callback cannot be used for VPN or multilink connections.**
   a. True
   b. False
4. **Which of the following statements is true? (Choose all that apply.)**
   a. RADIUS is used to authenticate users by default.
   b. Windows 2000 remote access systems support only IAS-supplied RADIUS.
   c. The RADIUS setting uses non-Windows 2000 user credentials to approve remote client access.
   d. Configuring remote access to use RADIUS requires a shared secret code.
5. **Which of the following is a secure configuration? (Choose all that apply.)**
   a. Callback on multilink connections
   b. Callback set by the user
   c. Caller ID
   d. Remote access account lockout enabled
   e. Windows authentication for logon

OBJECTIVES

3.10 Configure remote access protocols

REMOTE ACCESS AUTHENTICATION PROTOCOL • EAP • MS-CHAP • CHAP • SPAP • PAP

UNDERSTANDING THE OBJECTIVE

Windows 2000 supports several authentication protocols. Authentication protocols protect the user name and password transmitted from a client to the remote access server when submitted for logon.

WHAT YOU REALLY NEED TO KNOW

- Windows 2000 supports the following authentication protocols: **EAP**, MS-CHAP, MS-CHAP v2, CHAP, SPAP, and PAP.
- EAP is a PPP extension that allows third-party authentication solutions to endorse remote connections. Two solutions are included with Windows 2000: MD5 and smart card/certificate.
- CHAP is the industry standard of the remote access authentication protocols. It uses MD5 as its one-way encryption scheme to protect logon credentials. A new version, MS-CHAP v2, offers better encryption to protect credentials. CHAP is more secure than SPAP and PAP.
- MS-CHAP is an enhanced CHAP developed by Microsoft for the Windows platform. It uses one-way encryption to protect credentials. A new version, MS-CHAP v2, offers better encryption and fewer security holes due to removal of a few legacy conventions. MS-CHAP v2 is supported by Windows 2000 natively, Windows NT with Service Pack 4, Windows 98 with Service Pack 1, and Windows 95 through the **DUN** 1.3 upgrade through PPTP only (not PPP).
- SPAP is a reversible scheme used by Shiva remote access systems. SPAP is more secure than PAP.
- PAP uses plain text to transmit logon credentials.
- By default, Windows 2000 accepts only MS-CHAP and MS-CHAP v2 authentication methods from remote clients.

OBJECTIVES ON THE JOB

Configuring the authentication protocols for remote access connections is a simple act of enabling or disabling them. There are no configuration options available to fine-tune or adjust the supported authentication protocols. Additional EAP methods can be installed using the installation routine provided by a third-party method developer.

PRACTICE TEST QUESTIONS

1. **If all users log on using a biometric or an ID card instead of a password, which of the following authentication protocols is most likely to be used?**
    a. MS-CHAP
    b. EAP
    c. SPAP
    d. PAP
2. **Which of the following authentication protocols is enabled by default on Windows 2000? (Choose all that apply.)**
    a. EAP
    b. MS-CHAP v2
    c. MS-CHAP
    d. CHAP
    e. SPAP
    f. PAP
    g. Allow connections without authentication
3. **The PAP protocol offers no protection for the credentials transmitted by it.**
    a. True
    b. False
4. **Which authentication protocol is the most secure?**
    a. SPAP
    b. MS-CHAP
    c. CHAP
    d. PAP
5. **Which authentication protocol is the least secure?**
    a. SPAP
    b. MS-CHAP
    c. CHAP
    d. EAP
6. **Which authentication protocol relies on MD5? (Choose all that apply.)**
    a. SPAP
    b. MS-CHAP
    c. CHAP
    d. EAP
7. **Which of the following statements is true? (Choose all that apply.)**
    a. Windows 2000 can be configured so remote clients connect without authentication.
    b. Windows 2000, Windows NT, Windows 98, and Windows 95 support MS-CHAP v2 natively.
    c. Shiva uses a reversible encryption scheme.
    d. CHAP uses one-way encryption.

OBJECTIVES

3.11 Configure remote access encryption protocols

REMOTE ACCESS ENCRYPTION • DES • MPPE

UNDERSTANDING THE OBJECTIVE

Remote access connections can employ encryption to protect data transmitted between the client and server in addition to the protection provided by logon credentials and authentication.

WHAT YOU REALLY NEED TO KNOW

- Data can be encrypted over VPN links or over typical dial-up connections.
- VPN links encrypt all data transferred over them as a matter of course. PPTP performs this encryption automatically as a native feature of that protocol and communication method. L2TP supports data encryption through IPSec, but IPSec must be configured before it can be used. In addition, IPSec itself can be used outside of L2TP.
- Enabling data encryption on a remote access server is performed through a remote access profile (from within a remote access policy). Data encryption can be enabled (or supported) on the Encryption tab. There are three levels: no encryption, basic, and strong. Basic encryption uses **DES** (56-bit key) or **MPPE** (40-bit key). Strong encryption uses 3DES (three 56-bit keys) or MPPE (56-bit key). For data encryption to function, EAP, MS-CHAP, and/or MS-CHAP v2 must be enabled on the Authentication tab.
- Enabling data encryption on a remote access client is performed through the client's dial-up connection object. The Security tab must be configured with the Require secured password selection in the Validate my identity as follows pull-down list and the Require data encryption check box marked. The client attempts to use the highest encryption level supported by the remote access server.
- A second method of configuring the remote access client offers specific control over which encryption protocol is used. This is also configured from the Security tab; however, the Advanced (Custom Settings) option must be selected. By clicking the Settings tab, data encryption can be set to none, option, required, or maximum and the supported protocols can be individually enabled or disabled through check boxes.
- If the client and server do not both support the same or common authentication and encryption protocols, then the connection will not be allowed.

OBJECTIVES ON THE JOB

Data encryption is an important feature when interacting with sensitive and confidential information over publicly accessible communication lines. Configuring data encryption over every remote connection is a significant security improvement.

PRACTICE TEST QUESTIONS

1. **DIRK Inc. must protect its database, which is used by all of the employees on a daily basis. There are more than 30 remote clients that connect to the office LAN over telephone lines or VPN links. All of the remote clients are Windows 2000 Professional except for a single OS/2 system. Management decided that only MS-CHAP v2 should be supported on the remote access server and that only strong encryption is allowed. Which of the following must you do to comply with management's decision and still allow these remote systems to connect?**
   a. Select the Allow remote connections without authentication check box.
   b. Distribute a DES/3DES installation disk to all clients.
   c. Delete all remote access profiles.
   d. Make all remote systems Windows 2000.
2. **It turns out that the OS/2 computer system cannot support anything newer than Windows 98. What is the next step to making sure a Windows 98 system can connect to the DIRK Inc. LAN under the new connection rules?**
   a. Allow MS-CHAP.
   b. Enable connections without encryption.
   c. Prevent EAP connections.
   d. Install Service Pack 1.
3. **Data can be encrypted over typical dial-up connections, but not VPN links.**
   a. True
   b. False
4. **Which of the following statements is true? (Choose all that apply.)**
   a. VPN links encrypt all data transferred over them as a matter of course.
   b. PPTP performs encryption automatically as a native feature of the protocol and communication method.
   c. L2TP supports data encryption through DES.
   d. If the client and server do not both support the same or a common authentication and encryption protocol, then the connection will not be allowed.
5. **On a client system, which of the following can be configured? (Choose all that apply.)**
   a. Require encryption but allow the server to select the encryption protocol.
   b. Require a secured password but allow a connection without data encryption.
   c. Require a specific authentication protocol but allow a connection without data encryption.
   d. Require a specific authentication protocol but allow a connection with any level of data encryption if supported by the server.

Section 4

Installing, Configuring, Managing, Monitoring, and Troubleshooting Network Protocols in a Windows 2000 Network Infrastructure

OBJECTIVES

4.1 Install, configure, and troubleshoot network protocols

NETWORK PROTOCOL • TCP/IP • NWLINK • NETBEUI

UNDERSTANDING THE OBJECTIVE

Network protocols under Windows 2000 are easier to install, configure, manage, and troubleshoot than ever before. In most cases, after initial configuration, you'll never need to perform maintenance directly on the protocols.

WHAT YOU REALLY NEED TO KNOW

- Windows 2000 supports three native LAN protocols: TCP/IP, NWLink, and NetBEUI.
- NetBEUI is nonroutable and limited to 1024 hosts. While fast and efficient, it is not used on modern networks.
- NWLink is Microsoft's **IPX/SPX**-compatible protocol designed to support interaction with NetWare. NWLink is routable, but its use on modern networks is waning.
- TCP/IP is the most prominent protocol in the world, due to its use on the Internet. Windows 2000 (and all other Microsoft products) are designed to exploit TCP/IP as much as possible.
- All network components are installed and often configured through the Network and Dial-up Connections utility.
- Under TCP/IP, hosts are assigned IP addresses, whether statically or dynamically. Each IP address is a 32-bit number, which is used by the computer in binary form but viewed and managed by humans in dotted decimal notation (a set of four numbers between 0 and 255 separated by periods).
- The entire address space of TCP/IP is divided into subnets through the use of subnet masks, which are used by the computer to determine whether an IP address is within the current subnet or a different one. This determination is made by extracting the network ID and the host ID from the IP address.
- The TCP/IP address space is divided as follows:

Item	Class A	Class B	Class C
Initial Digits	0	10	110
Network IDs	126	16,328	2,097,150
Host IDs	16,777,214	65,534	254
Network Ranges	1.x.x.x-126.x.x.x	128.1.x.x-191.254.x.x	192.1.1.x-223.254.254.x
Class Subnet Mask	255.0.0.0	255.255.0.0	255.255.255.0

OBJECTIVES ON THE JOB

On modem networks, TCP/IP is the most prominent LAN protocol. However, NWLink (or IPX/SPX) is still common. Learning about the protocols your network uses is important for troubleshooting, capacity planning, and service deployment and configuration.

PRACTICE TEST QUESTIONS

1. **Which protocol is supported by Windows 2000 natively? (Choose all that apply.)**
   a. IPX/SPX
   b. NetBEUI
   c. TCP/IP
   d. Arc-Token
2. **Which utility is used in most cases to install and configure network components?**
   a. Network applet
   b. System applet
   c. Device Manager
   d. Network and Dial-up Connections
3. **TCP/IP is the second most prevalent protocol on the Internet.**
   a. True
   b. False
4. **Which of the following statements is true? (Choose all that apply.)**
   a. NetBEUI is nonroutable and limited to 1024 hosts.
   b. NWLink is not routable.
   c. IPX/SPX is Novell's duplicated protocol of Microsoft's original NWLink.
   d. NetBEUI is used on most networks.
   e. TCP/IP addresses can be assigned permanently or dynamically.
   f. A TCP/IP address is a 32-bit decimal number.
   g. A subnet mask is used to extract the network ID and host ID from an IP address.
5. **Which of the following apply to Class C addresses? (Choose all that apply.)**
   a. First three binary digits are 110
   b. Offers 254 hosts per class-level subnet
   c. Uses a subnet mask of 255.0.0.0
   d. Offers 16,328 network IDs
6. **Which of the following apply to Class B addresses? (Choose all that apply.)**
   a. First three binary digits are 0
   b. Offers 65,534 hosts per class-level subnet
   c. Uses a subnet mask of 255.255.255.0
   d. Offers 16,328 network IDs
7. **Which of the following applies to Class A addresses? (Choose all that apply.)**
   a. First three binary digits are 0
   b. Offers 254 hosts per class-level subnet
   c. Uses a subnet mask of 255.0.0.0
   d. Offers 2,097,150 network IDs

OBJECTIVES

4.2 Install and configure TCP/IP

TCP/IP • TCP/IP SETTINGS

UNDERSTANDING THE OBJECTIVE

TCP/IP is simple to install and, in most cases, simple to configure. The IP address, subnet mask, and default gateway settings are all that are required to communicate with a network. As the configuration of your network becomes more complex, TCP/IP can accommodate your needs by supporting multiple addresses, DNS servers, WINS servers, and other features.

WHAT YOU REALLY NEED TO KNOW

- TCP/IP is installed by default on Windows 2000. If it was not installed during initial setup of the operating system or was removed, it can be installed through any connection object from the Network and Dial-up Connections utility.
- By default, all interfaces (connection objects) using TCP/IP are set for automatic configuration.
- Through the Advanced button on the Internet Protocol (TCP/IP) Properties dialog box, you can access the Advanced TCP/IP Settings dialog box, which has four tabs:
  - IP Settings: define multiple IP addresses (with subnet mask) for this interface, additional default gateways (with its use metric), and this interface's use metric
  - DNS: define DNS servers, set the management method of non-FQDNs (append primary DNS suffixes, append parent DNS suffixes, or append custom DNS suffixes on order), define a DNS suffix for this interface, define whether to register this interface's IP configuration with DNS, and define whether to use this interface's DNS suffix for DNS registration
  - WINS: define WINS servers, enable LMHOSTS lookup, import LMHOSTS file, and set NetBIOS over TCP/IP use (enable, disable, as defined by DHCP)
  - Options: configure TCP/IP advanced options, including IPSec and TCP/IP Filtering. IPSec is used to create a secured communication tunnel between two IP addresses. Built-in filtering is used to allow all ports or to deny all ports but those specified.

OBJECTIVES ON THE JOB

Configuring TCP/IP should become second nature to anyone using Windows 2000 for networking or configuring Internet use on any level. On networks using DHCP, the defaults of automatic addressing eliminate client configuration. But on non-DHCP networks, TCP/IP supports complex configurations.

PRACTICE TEST QUESTIONS

1. **A company has a 100,000+ user network stationed in 39 primary customer countries across the world. Each of these networks is connected to one another over OC3 fiber-optic links. The networks support databases on every conceivable subject. Work tasks performed by one user often require interaction with more than 100 databases at a time. Each database is referred to by the FQDN assigned to its host server computer. There are seven DNS servers deployed within each LAN (in each country). Each LAN has a primary DNS server with two secondary DNS servers, and each secondary DNS server has two third-tier DNS servers. This layout is simply a result of the replication partnering defined by the system administrators. The DNS servers on a LAN are configured to communicate with one another, but they have no knowledge of DNS servers on remote LANs. Users have complained that they have difficulty getting to database systems hosted on other LANs, most likely due to the inability to resolve FQDNs to IP addresses. Which of the following is a possible solution to this problem?**
    a. Use DHCP to configure local DNS servers for all clients.
    b. Install WINS servers in each LAN.
    c. Configure DNS to forward unresolved queries to WINS.
    d. Define at least one DNS server from each LAN on the DNS tab of the Advanced TCP/IP Properties dialog box.
2. **After testing your proposed solution, you realize that performing a manual configuration on all clients is too much work. You develop a simpler plan. Which of the following requires the least amount of overall effort?**
    a. Install Windows 2000 Professional on all clients.
    b. Reconfigure all of the LANs to be part of a single Class A address space.
    c. Deploy DHCP on each LAN, configure it to provide clients with DNS server addresses from all LANs, and create a batch logon script to reconfigure each client to use DHCP.
    d. There is no simpler solution than manual reconfiguration of each client.
3. **When first installed or when a new connection object is created, TCP/IP is set by default to use DHCP.**
    a. True
    b. False
4. **Which of the following statements is true? (Choose all that apply.)**
    a. A single interface can have multiple IP addresses.
    b. Only a single DNS server can be defined for an interface.
    c. NetBIOS can be disabled on an interface.
    d. Each defined IP address has its own related subnet mask.
    e. Multiple WINS and DNS servers can be defined along with order of use.
    f. Data can be filtered using an Allow all but specific defined exceptions configuration.

OBJECTIVES

4.3 Install the NWLink protocol

NWLINK INSTALLATION

UNDERSTANDING THE OBJECTIVE

NWLink is a natively supported protocol of Windows 2000. It is often used on networks where Internet access is not required or when interaction with non-TCP/IP NetWare servers is required.

WHAT YOU REALLY NEED TO KNOW

- NWLink is not installed by default on Windows 2000, but it can be added to a system during or after initial installation.
- Installing NWLink after Windows 2000 has been installed takes place from within a connection object.
- Once NWLink is installed, it appears in the components list within every connection object. If the NWLink check box is selected, the protocol is enabled for that interface. If the NWLink check box is not selected, the protocol is disabled for that interface.
- On networks where only Windows 2000 is being used, NWLink does not require any configuration. On other networks, some configuration may be necessary. You configure NWLink by opening its properties dialog box from within a connection object. There are two settings:
  - Internal network number: An 8-digit hexadecimal number used to define a network ID number. This is used on multihomed systems connected to different networks; it improves the efficiency of packet routing. Unless you know otherwise, the default of 00000000 is sufficient.
  - Frame type: NWLink supports four frame types (Ethernet 802.2, Ethernet 802.3, Ethernet II, and Ethernet SNAP). On networks where only a single frame type is in use, Windows 2000 can auto-detect the frame type. But on networks where multiple frame types are in use, you must manually define the frame type(s) to use instead of relying upon auto-detect.

OBJECTIVES ON THE JOB

NWLink is a fast and efficient protocol compared to TCP/IP. It supports routing and does not require individual system addressing or complex configurations. However, NWLink does not support any of the Internet services; thus, it is used only when interaction with older NetWare servers is necessary.

PRACTICE TEST QUESTIONS

1. **DOPPEL Corp. decided to deploy a network to support the sharing of files and printers. There are more than 2000 computers that must be linked. They do not require access to the Internet. The person who will become the network administrator has a background only in desktop applications, not network management and control. Using self-configuring NICs and intelligent hubs, the network itself is successfully deployed. The clients use Windows 2000 Professional or Windows 98. A single Windows 2000 Server system is deployed to help centralize user accounts and resource access. Which of the following is the best choice for this network?**
   a. Deploy the TCP/IP protocol.
   b. Deploy the NetBEUI protocol.
   c. Deploy the NWLink protocol.
   d. Deploy the AppleTalk protocol.
2. **After further planning and discussion, DOPPEL Corp. decides to upgrade all systems to Windows 2000. Now which of the following is true?**
   a. The installed protocol needs no additional configuration.
   b. A DNS server must be deployed.
   c. The frame type must be specified.
   d. The Internet network number must be specified.
3. **NWLink manages the addressing of systems automatically so no manual addressing is necessary.**
   a. True
   b. False
4. **Which of the following statements is true? (Choose all that apply.)**
   a. NWLink is installed by default in Windows 2000.
   b. NWLink is used to access Internet services.
   c. NWLink can support access to NetWare servers.
   d. On a mixed NetWare environment, the frame types in use should be manually defined.
   e. The Internet network number is used to improve the efficiency of routing.
   f. When installed, NWLink is available on all connection objects.
5. **You must install and configure NWLink on a small 250-system network. There are many different systems on that network, including Windows 95, Windows 98, Windows NT, Windows 2000, and NetWare. Which of the following is the best configuration choice?**
   a. Manually set all systems to use the same frame type.
   b. Manually define an internal network number.
   c. Configure the systems to use all four available frame types.
   d. No manual configuration is necessary.
6. **NWLink can be enabled and disabled on a per-interface basis.**
   a. True
   b. False

OBJECTIVES

4.4 Configure network bindings

NETWORK BINDING

UNDERSTANDING THE OBJECTIVE

Network binding determines which networking components are allowed to interact. It also determines the order in which those interactions are allowed to occur.

WHAT YOU REALLY NEED TO KNOW

- Binding is the process of enabling one networking component to communicate with another.
- Bindings are defined on two levels—through a connection object and through the Advanced Settings dialog box of the Network and Dial-up Connection utility.
- Connection object-based binding focuses on enabling protocols and services over the network adapter or network interface of that connection object.
- The Adapters and Bindings tab lists the connection objects in one area and the protocol and service bindings for that connection object in another.
- Protocols are listed as subelements of each service for which binding is valid.
- Marking or clearing check boxes for protocols and services binds or unbinds those components from the interface.
- Setting binding for a protocol on one service does not affect that protocol's binding to other services.
- Binding settings only affect the selected network interface, not all connection objects.
- By default, when a new connection object is created, all possible bindings are enabled. Also, when a new networking component is installed, all possible bindings related to it are enabled.

OBJECTIVES ON THE JOB

Proper binding of network components can improve network performance, reduce timeout errors, and improve security. It is good practice to enable only those adapter-service-protocol relationships needed by your system.

PRACTICE TEST QUESTIONS

1. **Your Windows 2000 Server system has both NWLink and TCP/IP installed. The system has three network interfaces. Interface 1A is connected to a network comprised of older Novell systems. Interface 2B is connected to an intranet. Interface 3C is connected to the Internet. You need to configure bindings so only the required relationships between interfaces, services, and protocols are enabled. Which of the following settings should you make? (Choose all that apply.)**
   a. Enable all bindings on interface 1A.
   b. Disable NWLink on interface 3C.
   c. Disable Client for Microsoft Networks on interfaces 1A and 3C.
   d. Enable File and Printer Sharing for MS Networks on interfaces 1A and 2B.
   e. Disable TCP/IP on interface 2B.
   f. Disable Client for NetWare Networks on interfaces 2B and 3C.

2. **After you enabled only the required settings, the network administrator deployed several Windows 2000 servers in the Novell network. Which of the following changes should you now make to your system? (Choose all that apply.)**
   a. Enable Client for Microsoft Networks on interface 1A.
   b. Enable TCP/IP on interface 1A.
   c. Enable File and Printer Sharing for Novell Networks on interface 2B.
   d. Enable NWLink on interface 3C.

3. **Through which tool should you disable binding if you want to connect to a Microsoft network over TCP/IP but don't want to connect over NWLink?**
   a. The connection object's properties dialog box
   b. The Advanced Settings dialog box
   c. The Network applet
   d. The System applet

4. **Through which interface should you disable file and printer sharing to restrict all attempts to access your resources over the network?**
   a. The connection object's properties dialog box
   b. The Advanced Settings dialog box
   c. The Network applet
   d. The System applet

5. **Which of the following statements is true? (Choose all that apply.)**
   a. In the Advanced Settings dialog box, unbinding a protocol from one service removes it from all services.
   b. In the connection object's properties dialog box, unbinding a protocol removes it from all services.
   c. In the Advanced Settings dialog box, unbinding a protocol from one service does not affect other services.
   d. In the connection object's properties dialog box, unbinding a protocol does not remove it from all services.

OBJECTIVES

4.5 Configure TCP/IP packet filters

TCP/IP FILTERING • PORT NUMBER

UNDERSTANDING THE OBJECTIVE

TCP/IP filtering is the feature of the Windows 2000 TCP/IP protocol that limits, restricts, or prevents communications over TCP/IP. Filtering is an excellent tool for securing a system by preventing unwanted ports from being used.

WHAT YOU REALLY NEED TO KNOW

- TCP/IP filtering is disabled by default. When enabled, there are three areas of controls: TCP ports, UDP ports, and IP protocols. For each control area, there are only two settings: Permit All and Permit Only. Permit All allows any and all communications over the area to occur.
- Port numbers to TCP common services are:
  - FTP data (control) – 20 (21)
  - Telnet – 23
  - E-mail POP/SMTP – 25/110
  - Web (HTTP) – 80
  - NetBIOS – 139
- Port numbers for UDP common services include:
  - DNS queries – 53
  - NetBIOS name server – 137
  - SNMP – 161
  - RIP – 520
- Protocol numbers for common IP protocols include:
  - ICMP – 1
  - IGMP – 2
  - GGP – 3
  - IP in IP – 4
  - ST Stream – 5
  - TCP – 6
  - CBT – 7
  - EGP – 8

OBJECTIVES ON THE JOB

The filtering capabilities built into Windows 2000 TCP/IP should be used sparingly. They employ a simple Deny all but defined exceptions rule that is often difficult to fully configure for complex environments. Instead, deploy a true firewall product with an Allow all but defined exceptions rule.

PRACTICE TEST QUESTIONS

1. **Sore Loserman Corp. must control the traffic allowed into its Windows 2000 network from a contractor network with a dedicated link. The users on the contractor network should use Web services to interact with data on the SLC network, but network traffic scans reveal that FTP and Telnet sessions occur as well. Thinking this is a security breach at worst or a breach of contract at best, management demanded that you prevent all traffic but normal Web traffic from occurring, but they stipulated you cannot spend any additional budget funds on the solution. Which of the following would most likely result in a network configuration that meets the desires of management?**
   a. Configure DNS to reject all requests to systems that are not Web servers.
   b. Configure an IP protocol filter to Permit Only protocol 1.
   c. Remove the binding of the TCP/IP protocol from the interface with the contractor network.
   d. Configure a TCP port filter to Permit Only port 80.
2. **What should you do to reconfigure the system to allow for FTP traffic in addition to the traffic already allowed?**
   a. Disable filtering.
   b. Configure a UDP port filter to Permit Only ports 20 and 21.
   c. Configure a TCP port filter to Permit Only ports 20 and 21 (in addition to any other defined exceptions).
   d. Configure an IP protocol filter to Permit Only protocol 4 (FTP).
3. **By default, TCP/IP filtering is enabled but all of the area settings are Permit All.**
   a. True
   b. False
4. **Which of the following settings is supported by TCP/IP filtering, native to Windows 2000 TCP/IP protocol? (Choose all that apply.)**
   a. Allow all
   b. Allow all but defined exceptions
   c. Deny all
   d. Deny all but defined exceptions
5. **Which area or communication type can a TCP/IP filter be defined to control? (Choose all that apply.)**
   a. TCP traffic
   b. UDP traffic
   c. NetBIOS traffic
   d. IP protocol
   e. Source IP address
6. **When a TCP/IP filter is in use, administrators can bypass the denied ports or protocols by providing a user name and password.**
   a. True
   b. False

OBJECTIVES

4.6 Configure and troubleshoot network protocol security

IPSEC • SECURITY HOSTS • KERBEROS • KDC • TGT • TGS • VPN

UNDERSTANDING THE OBJECTIVE

Network protocol security focuses on using secure protocols to protect authentication credentials and all data communicated between systems (in other words, all network traffic). In relation to Windows 2000, this means working with IPSec, security hosts, Kerberos, and VPNs.

WHAT YOU REALLY NEED TO KNOW

- IPSec is a mechanism that creates a secure encrypted communication pipeline between two systems (with static IP addresses). IPSec can be used on a LAN, WAN, or across the Internet. All data transmitted within an IPSec pipeline is encrypted.
- Security hosts are authentication solutions deployed between remote access clients and the remote access server. The security hosts can be used to provide the identity of the client either upon connection before logging on to the network or at the same time as network logon.
- Pre-logon security hosts support such mechanisms as synchronized security cards. At logon, security hosts can support caller ID, callback security, smart card, biometric readers, or RADIUS.
- Kerberos is an authentication protocol used by Windows 2000 systems to protect logon credentials when communicating with a Windows 2000 domain controller. Kerberos is a complex system built into Windows 2000, but which functions invisibly to the user. Basically, upon providing your logon credentials, they are encrypted and sent to the domain controller. The domain controller communicates with the **KDC** to obtain a **TGT**—this is transmitted to your client. The client uses the TGT to request a **TGS**. If granted, the client uses the TGS to access resources and services.
- VPNs provide security through encrypting authentication and data transmitted over public or otherwise nonsecure networks, such as the Internet.
- Windows 2000 supports two VPN protocols: PPTP and L2TP. PPTP uses its own internal encryption mechanism to protect data. L2TP relies on IPSec.

OBJECTIVES ON THE JOB

Securing network connections is an important part of managing and maintaining any network. If your data is important enough to create and store, it's important enough to protect against damage and theft. Windows 2000 offers many methods of securing and protecting your data. It would be unwise not to take advantage of these built-in capabilities.

PRACTICE TEST QUESTIONS

1. **Which of the following security elements is enabled and present by default on Windows 2000 systems?**
    a. VPNs
    b. Security hosts
    c. IPSec
    d. Kerberos
2. **Which of the following is correct? (Choose all that apply.)**
    a. The domain controller requests a TGS, which is passed to the client.
    b. The client receives a TGT, which is used to request a TGS.
    c. The KDC issues the TGT, which is passed to the client.
    d. The TGT is used to access resources.
3. **IPSec can be used on a LAN, WAN, or across the Internet.**
    a. True
    b. False
4. **Which VPN protocol relies on IPSec for its security?**
    a. PPTP
    b. L2TP
    c. PPP
    d. MPPP
5. **Which type of security host (or security host feature) is supported natively within Windows 2000 (that is, configuration interfaces already exist in the operating system)? (Choose all that apply.)**
    a. RADIUS
    b. Biometrics
    c. Smart cards
    d. Caller ID verification
    e. Callback
    f. Synchronized security cards
6. **Which of the following can be used over the Internet? (Choose all that apply.)**
    a. L2TP
    b. PPTP
    c. Kerberos
    d. IPSec
7. **What is the only difference between a VPN link and a local area connection?**
    a. VPN links cannot print.
    b. VPN links require administrative access.
    c. VPN links usually have less bandwidth.
    d. VPN links don't support NetBIOS.

OBJECTIVES

4.7 Manage and monitor network traffic

NETWORK MONITOR • CAPTURE TRIGGER

UNDERSTANDING THE OBJECTIVE

Network Monitor is a native tool of Windows 2000 Server. It can be used to capture inbound and outbound traffic from a single system. Once captured, the contents of the packets can be examined.

WHAT YOU REALLY NEED TO KNOW

- Network Monitor is not installed by default.
- The Network Monitor driver is installed with the Network Monitor tool. The Network Monitor driver is needed to view Network Segment counters through System Monitor and to use **SMS**'s Network Monitor remotely on a system.
- Network Monitor can be used to capture any network packet transmitted over a NIC on the system. Network Monitor can view every detail of captured packets, but the original data cannot be reconstructed through this tool.
- Network Monitor can capture all traffic or only traffic matching a capture filter. Filter parameters can include traffic to or from a specific system, a specific protocol type, or packets containing a HEX or ASCII pattern string.
- Once captured, Network Monitor can use display filters to reduce the amount of data presented. Capture filter parameters can include specific system addresses, protocols, or protocol property values.
- A capture trigger can be used to initiate an audio signal, stop capture, or execute a batch file. Trigger events can be a combination of pattern matching and percentage of used buffer space.
- Packets are captured into a memory buffer that has a maximum of 8 MB less than the total amount of physical **RAM** in the computer.
- Captured packets can be saved for later review.
- Network Monitor can usually extract the host name of systems from data traffic.
- Network Monitor can be used to discover several issues, such as broadcasts or multicasts, use of restricted protocols or services, presence of rogue IP addresses, and use of clear-text logon credentials.
- Errors with protocols and network traffic in general are recorded as event details in the System Log (which is viewed through Event Viewer).

OBJECTIVES ON THE JOB

As a general rule, less is better on a network. Thus, remove any unneeded protocols and services. You should also consider reorganizing the layout of your resources to provide quick and easy access. You may even need to segment your network to reduce overall network chatter.

PRACTICE TEST QUESTIONS

1. **The FOPTG Group has a large network of more than 50,000 clients. Due to a recent security breach, all internal Web servers have been removed. A private Web site on the company intranet was distributing details about a research product, which should have remained fully confidential. Management asked you to monitor traffic to determine if any Web servers reappear on the network. Fortunately, there is no general Internet access and all e-mail traffic is routed through a border firewall. Your network is configured in four segments. A single Windows 2000 Server system serves as the router between these four segments. Which of the following actions results in a data set that indicates Web-related traffic?**
    a. Create a capture trigger to stop capture when the buffer is 75% full.
    b. Create a display filter to show only Web traffic.
    c. Create a capture filter to grab only HTTP traffic.
    d. Set a capture filter to retain only the header of packets.
2. **After taking this first action, you realize that you don't want to cause a serious performance drain on the routing server. Which of the following results in less performance hindrance but still supports your search requirements? (Choose all that apply.)**
    a. Set a capture buffer to only 4 MB.
    b. Capture only packet headers.
    c. Create a display filter to show only HTTP traffic.
    d. Create a capture trigger to stop capture when the ASCII pattern "Web" is found.
3. **The Network Monitor included with Windows 2000 Server is able to view traffic on any segment of the network.**
    a. True
    b. False
4. **Which of the following is an example or feature of data reduction supported by Network Monitor? (Choose all that apply.)**
    a. Capture filter
    b. Capture trigger
    c. Display filter
    d. Examine packet contents
5. **Which of the following statements is true? (Choose all that apply.)**
    a. Network Monitor can be used to determine when the deployment of WINS will improve network bandwidth availability.
    b. Network Monitor can be used to discover unapproved protocol use on the network.
    c. Network Monitor can be used to discover the IP address of a system in which a user account is logged on.
    d. Network Monitor can convert MAC addresses into host names.

OBJECTIVES

4.8 Enable, configure, and troubleshoot IPSec

IPSEC • DES • 3DES • L2TP

UNDERSTANDING THE OBJECTIVE

IPSec is the new breed of VPN security protocol. It is fully supported by Windows 2000 and will soon be the preferred VPN solution for all Microsoft products over PPTP.

WHAT YOU REALLY NEED TO KNOW

- IPSec is an end-to-end security mechanism. This means only the two systems communicating with each other using IPSec must know and understand IPSec. All systems in between need only support TCP/IP.
- All data transmitted between IPSec partners is fully encrypted.
- IPSec can function in two modes: transport mode and tunnel mode. However, tunnel mode is a unique use of IPSec, whereas all IPSec links create a tunnel between two endpoints.
- Data transmitted over an IPSec link is encrypted using either DES or 3DES. (The High Encryption Pack is required.)
- IPSec supports three types of secure authentication: Kerberos, public key certificates, and preshared keys. At least one common authentication method must be found to establish an IPSec link.
- The IPSec driver is an integral part of TCP/IP under Windows 2000. If the driver becomes corrupted or fails to function, then it can be replaced by removing and reinstalling TCP/IP.
- IPSec is used by L2TP to provide secure VPN communications. IPSec cannot be used with PPTP. L2TP/IPSec (or L2TP over IPSec) uses double encapsulation—L2TP encapsulates the PPP packet, and IPSec encrypts and encapsulates the packet.
- IPSec is implemented through policies. Policies are rules that govern how IPSec manages traffic. It is the policies themselves that enable or require security over IPSec point-to-point communications.

OBJECTIVES ON THE JOB

IPSec is currently the popular solution for creating secure links between two systems over WAN connections or the Internet. IPSec completely eliminates playback attacks, impersonation attacks, spoofing attacks, session hijacking attacks, and eavesdropping. Plus, with IPSec's versatility and wide range of customization options (through rules and filters), it can be easily adapted to match any system's security needs.

PRACTICE TEST QUESTIONS

1. **What is IPSec?**
    a. A subnetting tool used on TCP/IP networks
    b. A secure communication tool used to connect systems over insecure networks
    c. Internet Protocol Services exclusions list
    d. A new form of reply e-mail
2. **Which of the following statements is true? (Choose all that apply.)**
    a. IPSec is an end-to-end security mechanism.
    b. Only the two systems communicating with each other using IPSec must know and understand IPSec.
    c. All data transmitted between IPSec partners is fully encrypted.
    d. All routers between the two end clients must support IPSec.
3. **Data transmitted over an IPSec link is encrypted using either DES or 3DES.**
    a. True
    b. False
4. **What are the two modes in which IPSec can function?**
    a. Transparent
    b. Tunnel
    c. Trowel
    d. Transport
5. **IPSec is used with which remote access feature to provide secure communications?**
    a. PPTP
    b. L2TP
    c. MPPP
    d. SLIP
6. **Your system was attacked by a computer virus, which imposed some damage. You perform several system tests and discover that the only area in which problems are occurring is IPSec. You can communicate with the network—TCP/IP itself seems to function—but you are unable to establish IPSec links. What is your best course of action?**
    a. Reinstall Windows 2000.
    b. Remove and reinstall TCP/IP.
    c. Restart the IPSec Policy Agent.
    d. Run IPSECMON.
7. **IPSec is governed or controlled by:**
    a. Profiles
    b. Group membership
    c. Attribute settings
    d. Policies

OBJECTIVES

4.9 Configure IPSec for transport mode

IPSEC • L2TP IPSEC • TRANSPORT MODE

UNDERSTANDING THE OBJECTIVE

Using IPSec in transport mode establishes a secure communications link between two end systems. Use of IPSec in this manner is also known as L2TP/IPSec (or L2TP over IPSec). This mode of IPSec is the default operational mode for Windows 2000.

WHAT YOU REALLY NEED TO KNOW

- IPSec can function in two modes: transport mode and tunnel mode.
- In transport mode, a secure communications link is established between the sending and receiving systems. All data transmitted by either system is fully secure.
- When used in transport mode, TCP/IP (with IPSec support) must be the network protocol of both end clients.
- Transport mode is also known as client-to-client secured communications.
- Transport mode is enabled by default on Windows 2000 Server.
- Transport mode relies on the default IPSec policies to function. You can customize these policies or create your own to fine-tune your transport mode IPSec link.

OBJECTIVES ON THE JOB

Because L2TP/IPSec is enabled and supported by Windows 2000 simply by installing Routing and Remote Access, creating secure VPN links is fast and efficient. Numerous vendors, including major network access hardware providers, support L2TP. However, be aware that, because of incompatibilities between **IKE** and NAT, L2TP/IPSec cannot pass through typical Network Address Translators.

PRACTICE TEST QUESTIONS

1. **KILT Ltd. has a network with just over 2000 clients. The network is divided into seven subnets, but the entire network is housed within a single multistory building. The IRS is performing an audit of the company's financial records. Due to security restrictions, the auditor is not able to enter the financial records office and work from a network client system there. Instead, a new Windows 2000 Professional client system has been deployed in a locked room for the sole use of the auditor. You must grant secured access to the financial servers. Company policy requires that all transmissions to and from the financial servers be encrypted. Which of the following is your best choice to comply with this requirement?**
    a. Configure TCP/IP to encrypt all data.
    b. Use NWLink to connect.
    c. Use an IPSec tunnel mode link.
    d. Use an IPSec transport mode link.
    e. Disable Kerberos.
    f. Force use of e-mail encryption.
    g. Install the High Encryption Pack.

2. **What step is required to configure this link between the auditor's new client system and the financial server? (Choose all that apply.)**
    a. Install Routing and Remote Access on Windows 2000 Server.
    b. Install NetBIOS Gateway.
    c. Create a VPN connection object on the "client" system.
    d. Configure Routing and Remote Access on the "server" system to accept VPN connections.
    e. Grant the user account membership in the Administrators group.
    f. Create new IPSec policies.

3. **IPSec transport mode is enabled by default on Windows 2000.**
    a. True
    b. False

4. **Which of the following statements is true? (Choose all that apply.)**
    a. Using IPSec in transport mode establishes a secure communications link between two end systems.
    b. Use of IPSec on transport mode is also known as L2TP/IPSec (or L2TP over IPSec).
    c. Tunnel mode of IPSec is the default operational mode for Windows 2000.
    d. When used in transport mode, TCP/IP (with IPSec support) must be the network protocol of both end clients.
    e. Tunnel mode is also known as gateway-to-gateway secured communications.
    f. Transport mode relies on the default IPSec policies to function.
    g. L2TP/IPSec uses double encapsulation. First, L2TP encapsulates the PPP packet, and then IPSec encrypts and encapsulates the packet.

OBJECTIVES

4.10 Configure IPSec for tunnel mode

IPSEC • TUNNEL MODE

UNDERSTANDING THE OBJECTIVE

Using IPSec in tunnel mode establishes a secure connection between two networks. The data transmitted over the IPSec link is encrypted only between the two gateway systems on each network.

WHAT YOU REALLY NEED TO KNOW

- IPSec can function in two modes: transport mode and tunnel mode.
- In tunnel mode, IPSec is used to establish a communications gateway over the Internet (or other public insecure network) between two networks. Only the gateway systems must support IPSec. The secure communication link begins and ends with the gateway systems. Data transmission to the gateway from a client or from a server to the gateway is not secure.
- When used in tunnel mode, any network protocol can be used by the sender and receiver systems, because IPSec is not actually present on these systems. The end systems do not need to support IPSec, because the gateway systems create and support the secured tunnel.
- Tunnel mode is also known as gateway-to-gateway secured communications.
- In addition to defining the IPSec tunnel policy, you must have network communication between two networks, and each Windows 2000 Server system (the endpoints of the IPSec tunnel) must be configured to route their network's traffic across the IPSec link.

OBJECTIVES ON THE JOB

Using IPSec in tunnel mode offers a secure mechanism for two networks to exchange data. In a world of increasing security risks and greater value of information, protecting your network assets is important. Tunnel mode IPSec links offer a customized solution that is easily implemented and natively supported within Windows 2000.

PRACTICE TEST QUESTIONS

1. **FIRST RATE Inc. has two networks located on opposite sides of Los Angeles. Due to changes in job descriptions, management, and organization, the two networks must communicate on a more permanent basis. Previously, the networks were connected over a telephone dial-up connection every weekend to exchange data. The call was kept as short as possible due to long-distance toll charges. Now, a 24/7 connection of at least 128 KB is required to support the activity between the networks. You determine that DSL connections are the most cost-effective solution for the bandwidth. However, connecting the networks over the Internet poses a security problem. Which of the following is the best choice for linking these two networks together while maintaining security?**
   a. Use Web and FTP sites to exchange data.
   b. Use an IPSec tunnel mode link.
   c. Use an IPSec transport mode link.
   d. Use PPTP.
   e. Enable user-based encryption.
2. **What steps are required to configure this link between the two network locations over the Internet? (Choose all that apply.)**
   a. Install Routing and Remote Access on a Windows 2000 Server in each network.
   b. Define a filter with an IP Filter with a source address as a specific IP subnet. Be sure the mirroring check box is enabled and the Protocol tab is set to Any.
   c. Create a dial-up connection object on each network.
   d. Configure Routing and Remote Access on a server system in each network to accept incoming dial-up connections.
   e. Configure routing to use OSPF only.
   f. Create new IPSec policies.
   g. On the Tunnel Setting tab of the Rule Properties, define the tunnel endpoint using your IP address.
3. **When the tunnel mode IPSec links are used, only the gateway systems must support IPSec.**
   a. True
   b. False
4. **Which of the following statements is true? (Choose all that apply.)**
   a. Tunnel mode IPSec links are also known as client-to-client secured communications.
   b. In addition to defining the IPSec tunnel policy, each Windows 2000 Server gateway system must be configured to route its network's traffic across the IPSec link.
   c. In a tunnel mode configuration, data transmission to the gateway from a client or from a server to the gateway is not secure.
   d. In a tunnel mode configuration, only the gateways need to support IPSec.

OBJECTIVES

4.11 Customize IPSec policies and rules

IPSEC POLICIES • IPSEC RULES

UNDERSTANDING THE OBJECTIVE

IPSec is controlled through its policies. A policy is little more than a collection of rules. All traffic passing through an IPSec link is inspected; if it matches a rule, that rule's actions are applied to it.

WHAT YOU REALLY NEED TO KNOW

- An IPSec policy should be created before attempting to use IPSec on any system. The IPSec policy defines the rules that govern the security of the communication between the endpoints of an IPSec link.
- IPSec policies are created through an **MMC** snap-in. You must create your own interface by loading the IP Security Policy Management snap-in in a blank MMC. You should also select the policy's context: local system only, this domain, other domain, or other computer.
- There are three policies by default: Client (Respond Only)—use security only when requested; Server (Request Security)—always request security, but continue if unavailable; Secure Server (Require Security)—require security, and disconnect if unavailable
- Each policy consists of a collection of rules, the policy name, a description, how often to check for policy changes, and key exchange settings. Each rule consists of:
  - Whether to apply the rule to any tunnel or to a specific tunnel (identified by an endpoint IP address)
  - Whether to apply the rule to a network type: all, LAN, or remote access
  - Whether to apply the rule's authentication type: Kerberos, certificate, or preshared key
  - Whether to apply the rule based on an IP filter: source address, destination address, protocol used, or port used
  - The action to take if rules match with packet: permit insecure transmissions, request security, or require security
- Each IP filter consists of multiple filters; this allows for several subnets, addresses, and protocols to be combined into a single IP filter. Each filter can specify addresses by source and/or destination, protocol, or port.
- Filters are considered transport mode filters if the sender's or receiver's IP address is defined.

OBJECTIVES ON THE JOB

IPSec relies on policies to govern how it manages traffic. Policies can be defined using multiple filters to individual systems, groups of subnets, collections of protocols, and even specific communication ports. The more specific the filters, the more control a policy has over every aspect of network communication. When designing your policies and filters, keep in mind the goal of IPSec—to allow desired traffic and prevent unwanted traffic.

PRACTICE TEST QUESTIONS

1. **Which of the default IPSec policies can be used in an environment where insecure communications can occur? (Choose all that apply.)**
    a. Client (Respond Only)
    b. Server (Request Security Only)
    c. Secure Server (Require Security)
    d. None of the above
2. **Through what interface are IPSec policies defined?**
    a. Routing and Remote Access
    b. Network and Dial-up Connections
    c. IPSec MMC snap-in
    d. System applet
3. **Which of the following is a possible rule element within an IPSec policy? (Choose all that apply.)**
    a. Whether to apply the rule to any tunnel or to a specific tunnel
    b. Whether to apply the rule based on the operating system of the client
    c. Whether to apply the rule to a network type
    d. Whether to apply the rule based on group membership of the user
    e. Whether to apply the rule based on an IP filter
    f. Whether to apply the rule based on the timestamp of the communication
4. **An IPSec policy can be defined to apply to which of the following? (Choose all that apply.)**
    a. Local system only
    b. Operating system type
    c. This domain
    d. User group
5. **Each IP filter consists of multiple filters, which allows for several subnets, addresses, and protocols to be combined into a single IP filter. Each filter can specify addresses by source and/or destination, protocol, or port.**
    a. True
    b. False
6. **Which of the following statements is true? (Choose all that apply.)**
    a. Filters are considered transport mode filters if the sender's or receiver's IP address is defined.
    b. An IPSec policy should be created before attempting to use IPSec on any system.
    c. IPSec tunnel mode links are preconfigured by default for use.

OBJECTIVES

4.12 Manage and monitor IPSec

IPSEC MONITOR

UNDERSTANDING THE OBJECTIVE

IPSec management and monitoring is handled through several tools, including the IPSec MMC snap-in, IPSec Monitor, and Routing and Remote Access. These tools offer information about the existence of functioning IPSec links, but they don't offer information about the data being transmitted.

WHAT YOU REALLY NEED TO KNOW

- Through the IPSec MMC snap-in, use the Check Policy Integrity command in the All Tasks section of the Action menu to verify that changes made to IPSec policies are properly distributed through the group policy.
- Through the IPSec MMC snap-in, use the Restore Default Policies command to return the three default policies to their original configuration.
- Through the IPSec MMC snap-in, policies can be exported and imported.
- Launch the IPSec Monitor tool using the ipsecmon command from the Run command or command prompt. This tool displays active secure sessions (listing source and destination addresses, protocols, ports, and so on) and session statistics (bytes transmitted, failed packets, packets not encrypted, packets not authenticated, and so on).
- Event details related to IPSec are recorded in either the Security Log or the System Log. These logs are viewed through Event Viewer.
- IPSec is implemented as a remote access link, and therefore some information about IPSec links is obtained through the Routing and Remote Access utility. Through the Ports folder, you can view statistics and status of the L2TP ports. In addition, Remote Access Logging records IPSec-related events.
- If IPSec security associations fail, you may need to restart the IPSec Policy Agent through the Services tool.
- If IPSec secure links continue to fail, double-check that both endpoints support the same encryption and authentication methods. Then, double-check all policies, rules, and filters. In some cases, you may need to delete and re-create a policy.

OBJECTIVES ON THE JOB

IPSec is completely invisible to the end user. To determine whether IPSec is being used, view the status of the links through IPSec Monitor or the Routing and Remote Access utility's Ports folder. Once properly configured, IPSec offers an efficient, secure solution for connecting two systems over insecure networks.

PRACTICE TEST QUESTIONS

1. **JORT Group recently fired its network administrator. You've been hired as his replacement. Your first task is to re-enable the IPSec link between the JORT network and the PORK Inc. network, which has been offline since before the last network administrator was hired. You examine the long list of IPSec policies through the IPSec MMC snap-in. You realize that there are several redundant policies, many of which are either unnecessary or contradict other settings. What step should you take to restore an IPSec link in this situation? (Choose all that apply.)**
   a. Reinstall Windows 2000.
   b. Install Routing and Remote Access.
   c. Restore default policies.
   d. Delete all custom policies.
   e. Remove, then reinstall TCP/IP.
2. **After performing this first step, you review the requirements for the link and create your own IPSec policies. Before testing the link, you should perform which of the following actions to make sure your changes have taken effect?**
   a. Stop and restart the remote access service.
   b. Issue the Check Policy Integrity command.
   c. Review the logs through Event Viewer.
   d. Launch IPSec Monitor.
3. **Even after performing your last chosen action, the IPSec link fails to initiate. You carefully review the policies and all filters. You also test the network connections. What is another useful action you should perform in attempting to jump-start the IPSec link?**
   a. Stop and restart the IPSec Policy Agent service.
   b. Export your IPSec policies.
   c. Enable logging through Routing and Remote Access.
   d. Capture traffic with Network Monitor.
4. **Event details related to IPSec may be recorded in both the Security Log and the System Log.**
   a. True
   b. False
5. **What tool can be used to view active sessions and general IPSec statistics?**
   a. Routing and Remote Access
   b. IPSec Monitor
   c. System Monitor
   d. Network Monitor
6. **If an IPSec link fails to initiate, it is possible that the end clients don't share a common authentication method.**
   a. True
   b. False

Section 5

Installing, Configuring, Managing, Monitoring, and Troubleshooting WINS in a Windows 2000 Network Infrastructure

OBJECTIVES

5.1 Install and configure WINS

WINS

UNDERSTANDING THE OBJECTIVE

WINS is a name resolution system that converts NetBIOS host names into IP addresses. WINS should be used to reduce the amount of bandwidth consumed by typical NetBIOS broadcast name resolution.

WHAT YOU REALLY NEED TO KNOW

- WINS is not required in pure Windows 2000 environments (native mode), because all resolution issues are handled by AD or DNS, not NetBIOS.
- WINS is installed through the Network and Dial-up Connections tool, and configured through the WINS tool located in Administrative Tools.
- After the WINS service is installed on a Windows 2000 Server system (with a static IP address), each client must be configured (either manually or through DHCP) to use WINS by defining the IP address of one or more WINS servers.
- WINS maintains its mapping database automatically, but static mappings can be defined. These require system name, optional NetBIOS scope, type (unique, group, domain name, Internet group, or multihomed), and IP address.

OBJECTIVES ON THE JOB

WINS is the preferred host name resolution service for large and medium-sized mixed Microsoft operating system networks. Once installed and configured, WINS significantly reduces the amount of broadcast traffic on a network. WINS is the second step in NetBIOS name resolution.

PRACTICE TEST QUESTIONS

1. **VORK Inc., a scientific research firm, recently expanded its network from 300 clients to more than 1200. They also added 30 servers to support the various network applications used by employees. The operating systems are mostly Microsoft Windows, but they include Windows 95, 98, NT, 2000, and Me. Each client has the ability to share data with every other client on the network to help promote cross-discipline exploration. Thus, each client may share folders or support a Web site. Network administrators have been closely monitoring the amount of data transmitted over the network in relation to broadcasts and other supporting communications. They discovered that, as more clients offer shared resources on the network, less actual data is transmitted between systems compared to the level of network traffic. In fact, most of the current network traffic seems to be broadcast traffic. Which of the following solutions results in the greatest recovery of network bandwidth for actual data transmission?**
   a. Deploy a faster network technology (such as Gigabit Ethernet or fiber-optic).
   b. Set all clients to M-node operation.
   c. Deploy WINS servers.
   d. Force all systems to use Windows NT.
2. **After deploying your choice, no noticeable change occurred in network traffic. You verify that all WINS servers are properly installed. What configuration item was most likely forgotten in the deployment of WINS?**
   a. Defining a backup path
   b. Setting a pull replication interval
   c. Defining replication partners
   d. Configuring clients
3. **All the name-to-IP-address mappings maintained by WINS are static.**
   a. True
   b. False
4. **Which of the following statements is true? (Choose all that apply.)**
   a. WINS is required in pure Windows 2000 environments.
   b. Windows 2000 networks use Active Directory or DNS for name resolution.
   c. Clients can have multiple WINS servers defined.
   d. WINS reduces network broadcast traffic.
5. **Windows Internet Naming Service is used to perform which of the following?**
   a. Assign IP configuration to clients.
   b. Resolve FQDN to IP addresses.
   c. Resolve host names to IP addresses.
   d. Control traffic patterns across a network.

OBJECTIVES

5.2 Configure WINS replication

WINS REPLICATION • PUSH • PULL

UNDERSTANDING THE OBJECTIVE

Multiple WINS servers are deployed to provide fault tolerance and load balancing. Replication ensures that each WINS server has a current mappings database.

WHAT YOU REALLY NEED TO KNOW

- Each WINS server can be configured for push or pull.
- In the pull configuration, the server receives updates from other servers. This configuration is time-based. Also, a persistent connection can be created to allow for real-time updates.
- In the push configuration, the server sends updates to other servers. This configuration is event-based, such as when the service starts or when mappings change.
- Configuring replication requires that each WINS server's replication configuration be defined, and then replication partners must be defined and configured.
- Setting a WINS server's replication configuration is done through the properties dialog box of the Replication Partners folder.
- Issuing the New Replication Partner from the Replication Partners folder creates push or pull partners. After providing the partner's name or IP address, it is automatically configured as both push and pull.
- Opening a partner's properties dialog box enables you to set the partner to push, pull, or push/pull replication along with enabling persistent connections, start times, intervals, and a number of changes to initiate replication settings.
- Three common scenarios for replication partnerships are:
  1. Designate a primary WINS server—all others replicate with the primary.
  2. Create a logical circle of WINS server partners, so that A is a partner with B, B with C, C with D, and D with A.
  3. Create a logical linear configuration of partners, so that A is a partner with B, B with C, C with D, and D with E.

OBJECTIVES ON THE JOB

Both systems in a replication relationship must be configured for the same type of replication—push or pull. Microsoft recommends that you configure each partner to support both push and pull to allow for all possible means of replication.

PRACTICE TEST QUESTIONS

1. **FILK Group has a network of more than 4000 systems, including Windows 98, NT, and 2000. They deployed nine WINS servers and configured all of the clients to use WINS for NetBIOS name resolution. Each client used the WINS server located in his or her subnet. During a regular network health check, the system administrator discovered that accessing systems in other subnets was difficult when host names were used. What is the most likely cause of the difficulty?**
    a. Name resolution services cannot function across subnets.
    b. WINS replication is not configured.
    c. A backup of the WINS database file has become corrupted.
    d. The WINS service has been stopped.
2. **To aid in resolving this problem, which of the following would be the most cost-effective solution and the best solution according to Microsoft?**
    a. Deploy WINS proxy agents.
    b. Upgrade all systems to Windows 2000.
    c. Configure replication partners.
    d. Manually create static mappings for all systems in alternate subnets on each WINS server.
3. **Microsoft recommends configuring all WINS servers as both pull and push partners.**
    a. True
    b. False
4. **Which type of replication is initiated on a time interval?**
    a. Pull
    b. Push
    c. Symmetrical
5. **When creating partnerships between two WINS servers, which of the following should be true? (Choose all that apply.)**
    a. Configure both systems for push/pull.
    b. Configure both systems for push.
    c. Configure one system for push and one for pull.
    d. Configure both systems for pull.
6. **Which of the following replication partnership layouts provides obvious primary and secondary WINS servers?**
    a. A-B, A-C, A-D, A-E, A-F
    b. A-B, B-C, C D, D-E, E-F
    c. A-B, B-C, C-D, D-E, E-F, F-A
    d. A-B, C-D, E-F
7. **WINS can be configured to automatically create replication partners on smaller networks.**
    a. True
    b. False

OBJECTIVES

5.3 Configure NetBIOS name resolution

NETBIOS NAME RESOLUTION • B-NODE • P-NODE • M-NODE • H-NODE

UNDERSTANDING THE OBJECTIVE

On networks in which non-Windows 2000 Microsoft operating systems are in use, NetBIOS name resolution takes place. NetBIOS name resolution is the process by which a host name is resolved into an IP address.

WHAT YOU REALLY NEED TO KNOW

- Systems can communicate with other systems on a network through two means: broadcast or directed. Broadcast communications is the default for most systems; directed communications must be enabled and configured. Only direct messages can cross routers. WINS was designed specifically as a directed resolution solution.
- Microsoft clients must use one of four name resolution mechanisms, known as node types:
  - B-node (broadcast): sends only broadcast messages
  - P-node (point-to-point): direct communication with a WINS server only
  - M-node (modified): a hybrid mechanism that attempts broadcast first, then attempts direct communication
  - H-node (hybrid): a hybrid mechanism that attempts direct communication first, then attempts broadcast
- Windows WINS clients are configured for H-node operation. You can verify this by issuing the ipconfig /all command from the command prompt and viewing the Node Type setting.
- When in H-node, the NetBIOS name resolution process is as follows:
  1. Local NetBIOS name cache
  2. Primary WINS server
  3. Secondary WINS server(s)
  4. B-node broadcasts
  5. LMHOSTS file
  6. HOSTS file
  7. DNS server

OBJECTIVES ON THE JOB

Windows clients typically use B-node by default, and then H-node when configured to use WINS. A Registry setting can be used to enable P-node or M-node, but this is typically not recommended.

PRACTICE TEST QUESTIONS

1. **By default, Windows 98 is configured to perform name resolution for host names in what manner?**
   a. LMHOSTS
   b. Broadcast
   c. Direct
   d. M-node
2. **After a Windows client is configured to use WINS servers, which node type is used for its name resolution?**
   a. B-node
   b. P-node
   c. M-node
   d. H-node
3. **Operating systems that use NetBIOS name resolution and are not configured to use WINS servers will use P-node name resolution by default.**
   a. True
   b. False
4. **Put the following elements of the H-node NetBIOS name resolution process in order:**
   a. HOSTS file
   b. Primary WINS server
   c. B-node broadcasts
   d. DNS server
   e. Local NetBIOS name cache
   f. LMHOSTS file
   g. Secondary WINS server(s)
5. **Which command displays the node type a system is using for name resolution?**
   a. ipconfig /all
   b. wins /show
   c. nbstat –a
   d. net show resolve
6. **Which node type attempts a broadcast resolution first, and then only uses a direct communication if the broadcast fails?**
   a. B-node
   b. P-node
   c. M-node
   d. H-node
7. **Which type or part of communication can pass from one subnet to another? (Choose all that apply.)**
   a. B-node
   b. P-node
   c. M-node, first attempt
   d. H-node, first attempt

OBJECTIVES

5.4 Troubleshoot WINS

WINS TROUBLESHOOTING

UNDERSTANDING THE OBJECTIVE

Most WINS troubleshooting is preventive maintenance. In addition, only through correct maintenance are WINS disaster recovery methods available.

WHAT YOU REALLY NEED TO KNOW

- If a name resolution fails:
  1. Check network connectivity between the client and the WINS server.
  2. Check network connectivity with the resolved name's IP address.
  3. Restart the WINS service or reboot the WINS server host system.
  4. Delete the name mapping and reboot the owner system.
  5. Stop the WINS service, replace the WINS database with a backup (using the Restore Database command from the Action menu of the stopped WINS server), and then restart the service.
- Replacing the WINS database with a backup requires that a backup exist. WINS can maintain its own backup if you define a path for it on the General tab of the server's properties dialog box. You should also mark the check box for Back up database during server shutdown.
- A WINS database backup can be manually initiated by issuing the Back Up Database command, then providing a destination for the backup files (including WINS.MDB).
- Compacting the database improves performance and aids in maintaining a corruption-free database. Compacting can only be performed from a command-line utility. This process can be automated using a scheduled batch file.
- Scavenging the database is a process by which out-of-date name-to-IP-address mappings are removed from the database. This command should be used on a regular basis to prune the database of useless information.
- Testing a WINS server for proper name-to-IP-address mappings can be performed by issuing a ping command using a system's name from the command prompt and viewing the results. If a mapping exists, the IP address is used to perform the ping. You now only need to verify that the IP address returned matches that of the intended system.

OBJECTIVES ON THE JOB

Troubleshooting WINS is a fairly straightforward endeavor. If things don't function as planned, you simply restart the service and/or the system, remove the offending mappings, or restore the backup database. If all else fails, most likely something other than WINS is not functioning properly.

PRACTICE TEST QUESTIONS

1. **The SKIRL Corp. network experienced several power fluctuations during a thunderstorm over the weekend. On Monday morning, as users begin logging on to the network and attempting to access resources, they discover that some attempts fail. You perform several tests to access resources from several clients and determine that WINS is not properly resolving host names. Which of the following is a valid course of action in your attempt to resolve this issue? (Choose all that apply.)**
   a. Check network connectivity between the client and the WINS server.
   b. Reinstall Windows 2000 Server.
   c. Check network connectivity with the resolved name's IP address.
   d. Manually define static mappings for all failed resolutions.
   e. Delete the name mapping and reboot the owner system.
   f. Define push/pull partners.
   g. Restart the WINS service or reboot the WINS server host system.
2. **After performing all the possible troubleshooting options, you decide the WINS database itself has become corrupted. Which of the following is a valid and minimal step in restoring the database?**
   a. Uninstall the WINS service.
   b. Manually re-create all static mappings.
   c. Use the Restore Database command.
   d. Deploy a new primary WINS server.
3. **Although not enabled by default, WINS can maintain its own backup when properly configured.**
   a. True
   b. False
4. **Through what mechanism can the WINS database be compacted? (Choose all that apply.)**
   a. The command line
   b. The WINS MMC snap-in
   c. A batch file
   d. The properties dialog box for the WINS server
5. **The scavenge command performs what operation?**
   a. Searches the network for new systems
   b. Forces a replication
   c. Pulls mapping data from the NetBIOS name cache
   d. Removes invalid mappings
6. **What command or tool can be used to quickly determine if WINS is properly returning the correct IP address for a resolved host name?**
   a. View the HOSTS file.
   b. Use the ping command.
   c. Use Telnet.
   d. Open the System Information tool.

OBJECTIVES

5.5 Manage and monitor WINS

WINS MANAGEMENT • WINS MONITORING

UNDERSTANDING THE OBJECTIVE

WINS is a self-sustaining name resolution service, but there are several monitoring and management tasks you can perform to improve its reliability over time. These range from inspecting its current operation to verifying the database records.

WHAT YOU REALLY NEED TO KNOW

- Issuing the Display Server Statistics command from the Action menu when the server name is selected allows you to see current WINS activity statistics.
- The Active Registrations folder contains all current name mappings and provides information, such as record type, IP address, state, static, owner, version, and expiration.
- The Replication Partners folder contains defined replication data.
- Verification of database consistency and version ID consistency can be initiated from the Action menu of the WINS server. These actions check that each entry in the database is current and properly defined on each WINS server.
- Push or pull replications can be manually initiated through the Action menu of the WINS server.
- The All Tasks area of the WINS server's Action menu offers the commands to start, stop, pause, resume, and restart the WINS service.
- The operation of WINS can be monitored through System Monitor by viewing counters from the WINS Server object.
- If there are non-WINS-enabled operating systems on the network that need NetBIOS name resolution, you can use the WINS proxy agent to manage their requests. The WINS proxy agent intercepts the broadcast request (which the WINS server does not) and communicates with the WINS server on behalf of the non-WINS client.
- WINS proxy agent is enabled on Windows 2000 servers through the Registry by adding the EnableProxy value entry.

OBJECTIVES ON THE JOB

Monitoring WINS operations is typically not required. Other than searching for known problems or evaluating system efficiency, you'll have little need to oversee the operation of WINS. However, regular maintenance (scavenging, consistency checks, backups, and so on) ensures the longevity of your WINS infrastructure.

PRACTICE TEST QUESTIONS

1. **DLIP Ltd. recently deployed several WINS servers on its network. After the deployment, the amount of network bandwidth used for actual data transmission greatly increased, which resulted in more clients sharing resources. None of the Windows operating systems is having a problem accessing resources, but the UNIX, Linux, and OS/2 systems are slow in connecting to resources. In order to improve resource access for these non-Windows clients, what should you do?**
    a. Deploy additional WINS servers in a secondary server capacity.
    b. Redefine the partner replication layout from a star to a circle topology.
    c. Deploy WINS proxy agents.
    d. Restrict non-Windows operating system use.
2. **WINS servers can respond directly to broadcast requests for name resolutions.**
    a. True
    b. False
3. **Which of the following statements is true? (Choose all that apply.)**
    a. Push and pull replication processes can be manually initiated.
    b. The Active Registrations folder only displays dynamic mappings, not static mappings.
    c. The WINS service can only be stopped, paused, and restarted through the service applet.
    d. The consistency of the database can be tested through two manually initiated verifications.
    e. The status of WINS operation can only be viewed through System Monitor.
4. **Which of the following is a useful task in maintaining the reliability of WINS? (Choose all that apply.)**
    a. Maintaining database backups
    b. Regularly scavenging
    c. Regularly performing consistency checks
    d. Enabling replication partners
    e. Testing for network broadcasts
    f. Checking the System Log for events related to WINS
    g. Monitoring the workload of each WINS server
5. **Through System Monitor, where are measurements related to WINS primarily located?**
    a. WINS Client object
    b. WINS Server object
    c. System object
    d. NetBIOS Resolution object

Section 6

Installing, Configuring, Managing, Monitoring, and Troubleshooting IP Routing in a Windows 2000 Network Infrastructure

OBJECTIVES

6.1 Install IP routing protocols

IP ROUTING PROTOCOL • ROUTE • NETSH • RIP • OSPF

UNDERSTANDING THE OBJECTIVE

Routing protocols enable complex can changing network environments to maintain efficient and fault-tolerant delivery of network packets. Routing protocols transform static routing systems into dynamic systems, which are updated as the network changes. Windows 2000 supports IP and IPX routing, but only IP routing is covered on the exam.

WHAT YOU REALLY NEED TO KNOW

- Routing is configured through the Routing and Remote Access tool and the ROUTE and NETSH command-line tools.
- Routing is an integral part of Windows 2000; it only needs to be enabled (not installed).
- At least two interfaces should be present before enabling routing.
- Routing protocols are used to dynamically update multiple routers on a network in order to provide the most efficient delivery of network traffic.
- Windows 2000 has two installable IP routing protocols: **RIP** (a distance vector protocol) and **OSPF** (a link-state routing protocol).
- Once installed, the IP routing protocol will appear under the IP Routing section.
- After installation of the protocol, it must be manually bound to interfaces. In order for a routing protocol to function, it must be bound to at least two interfaces.

OBJECTIVES ON THE JOB

The use of dynamic IP routing protocols such as RIP and OSPF have greatly simplified the burden of maintaining static routing tables. RIP and OSPF allow routers to communicate with each other to exchange and update routing tables. When all routers have the correct and current information in their routing tables, the network is considered to be "converged." The process of updating the tables is known as "convergence." The ultimate goal of a routing protocol is to maintain convergence by consuming the least amount of bandwidth within the shortest time frame of each convergence activity.

PRACTICE TEST QUESTIONS

1. **VRAH Inc. has a network of 460 clients. It is divided into two segments of approximately 230 clients each, with about 10 servers in each segment. The segments are connected through a single Windows 2000 Server system, which has a network interface in each subnet. Routing and Remote Access has been configured to act as a network router on this connecting system. Which of the following actions must be performed in order for traffic from one segment to reach the other segment?**
    a. Install RIP
    b. Install OSPF
    c. Configure demand-dial routing
    d. No other configuration change is necessary
2. **VRAH Inc. has grown considerably. The network now consists of 17 segments with Windows 2000 servers used to connect adjacent segments. Some of these connecting servers are linked to two segments, while others connect to three or four. Routing and Remote Access has been configured to act as a network router on each connecting server. Which of the following actions can be performed to enable traffic from one segment to reach the other segment in the most efficient manner possible? (Choose all that apply.)**
    a. Install RIP
    b. Install OSPF
    c. Configure demand-dial routing
    d. No other configuration change is necessary
3. **Routing and protocols are needed only when two or more routers are present on a network.**
    a. True
    b. False
4. **Which of the following steps should be performed to transform a Windows 2000 Server system with NICs in two or more segments into a dynamic router? (Choose all that apply.)**
    a. Enable routing
    b. Install Routing and Remote Access services
    c. Enable NAT
    d. Install an IP routing protocol
    e. Bind interfaces to the routing protocol
5. **Which of the following statements is true? (Choose all that apply.)**
    a. Routing is enabled by default on Windows 2000.
    b. Routing protocols are needed when two or more routers are present on a network.
    c. At least three interfaces must be present before installing routing protocols.
    d. Routing protocols are bound by default to all available interfaces.
    e. A routing protocol must be bound to at least two interfaces to function.

OBJECTIVES

6.2 Configure IP routing protocols

IP ROUTING PROTOCOL

UNDERSTANDING THE OBJECTIVE

RIP's defaults are sufficient for most situations, but its configuration can be customized. OSPF requires configuration before it can be used. Windows 2000 supports RIPv2, which is a superset of RIPv1. RIPv2 offers many of the features and benefits of OSPF. RIPv1 routers read only the RIPv1 information and discard all RIPv2 data. RIP is a flexible IP routing protocol, but OSPF is built for very large networks (such as routers with greater than 15 hops).

WHAT YOU REALLY NEED TO KNOW

- After interfaces have been bound for the IP routing protocol, there are two levels of configuration: on the top-level routing protocol folder under IP Routing, and on the bound interface.
- RIP's configuration settings include: maximum update delay, logging, and announcement control (accept or ignore updates).
- OSPF's configuration settings include: interface IP, enable autonomous system boundary router, logging, defining OSPF areas, defining virtual interfaces, and route update management (only if autonomous system boundary router is enabled).
- Each RIP interface offers the following configuration settings: auto-static or period update mode, outgoing packet control (RIP v1 broadcast, v2 broadcast, v2 multicast, or silent RIP), incoming packet control (RIP v1 and v2, v1, v2, ignore all), route cost, route tagging, authentication activation w/password, route update management, how to interact with neighboring RIP routers, announcement interval, route expire time, route remove time, split-horizon processing, poison-reverse processing, trigger updates, using clean-up updates when stopping, using host routes as announcements, using default routes in announcements, and disabling subnet summarization.
- Each OSPF interface offers the following configuration settings: enable OSPF, select area ID, set router priority, set cost, set password, set network type (broadcast, point-to-point, nonbroadcast multiple access), define **NBMA** neighbors and priority, transit delay, retransmit interval, Hello interval, Dead interval, poll interval, and maximum transmission unit size.
- Silent RIP is a setting used to allow a router to accept updates and announcements from other routers, but none are sent out.

OBJECTIVES ON THE JOB

Routing is a complex subject. Microsoft objectives fail to provide enough detail for the depth of knowledge required to understand routing, much less pass the exam. The layout of these objectives is not sufficient to define and explain every aspect of IP routing protocol configuration. Please consult the Windows Resource Kit for in-depth discussions of RIP, OSPF, and routing in general.

PRACTICE TEST QUESTIONS

1. **Routing configuration can take place in the following areas:**
    1. RIP top-level routing protocol
    2. OSPF top-level routing protocol
    3. RIP interface
    4. OSPF interface

   Match the following configuration settings with each location where it can be made:
    a. Update or transmit delay
    b. Logging
    c. Ignore updates
    d. Autonomous system boundary router
    e. Define virtual interfaces
    f. Auto-static mode
    g. Incoming and outbound packet control
    h. Router priority
    i. Set network type to NBMA

2. **Which of the following statements is true? (Choose all that apply.)**
    a. OSPF can be used immediately after binding surfaces.
    b. RIP can be used immediately after binding surfaces.
    c. RIP can support networks with more than 15 hops.
    d. OSPF can support networks with more than 15 hops.
    e. RIPv2 can be used to communicate with RIPv1 routers.
    f. Silent RIP is a setting used to allow a router to accept updates and announcements from other routers, but none are sent out.

3. **When configuring an OSPF interface, which of the following is a valid option for a network type? (Choose all that apply.)**
    a. Point-to-point
    b. Broadcast
    c. Multicast
    d. NBMA

4. **Which of the following is a valid setting for a RIP interface? (Choose all that apply.)**
    a. Outgoing packet control (ignore all)
    b. Outgoing packet control (RIP v2 broadcast)
    c. Incoming packet control (RIP v1 and 2)
    d. Outgoing packet control (silent RIP)
    e. Incoming packet control (v2 multicast)
    f. Incoming packet control (RIP v1)

5. **RIP interfaces can be configured to use split horizon processing and poison-reverse processing.**
    a. True
    b. False

OBJECTIVES

6.3 Troubleshoot IP routing protocols

IP ROUTING PROTOCOL TROUBLESHOOTING

UNDERSTANDING THE OBJECTIVE

Routing using RIP or OSPF is a dynamic process. As the network evolves, so does the routing information. Once properly configured, Windows 2000 routers function without maintenance, but when problems occur, most of the solutions are manual.

WHAT YOU REALLY NEED TO KNOW

- All possible hardware problems should first be eliminated. Check name resolution processes (DNS and WINS), as well as IP configurations, especially gateways, on all affected systems.
- You should work from either end of the communication (sender or recipient) and work forwards or backward to locate the point of failure.
- Routing tables should be checked with the route print command.
- The ping, pathping, tracert, and arp-a commands, as well as Network Monitor, can be used to verify communications between systems.
- Router configuration and routing protocol configuration should be checked.
- Keep the following items in mind when reviewing the system:
  - Silent RIP routers do not transmit route information to other routers.
  - RIP can support up to 15 hops; otherwise, you get a Destination Unreachable error.
  - Verify that RIPv2 routers are using broadcasts, not multicasts, if RIPv1 routers are present.
  - All routers using authentication should use the same password.
  - On OSPF routers, the Dead interval should be at least four times the Hello interval (10 seconds by default).
  - All neighboring OSPF routers must use the same authentication setting (on/off), password, Hello interval, Dead interval, Area ID, and stub setting.
  - All OSPF router IDs must be unique.
  - Each OSPF routed area must have a designated router with a Router Priority Level of 0 or greater.
- All routers that communicate with each other must run the same IP routing protocol (RIP or OSPF).

OBJECTIVES ON THE JOB

In most cases, router or routing problems are faulty physical connections or human errors in configuration. A systematic approach to the situation is often the only means of discovering the problem. Unfortunately, there are no all-encompassing troubleshooting or even trouble-detection tools for routing. You must employ several TCP/IP tools and a lot of manual inspection.

PRACTICE TEST QUESTIONS

1. **RIP and OSPF, although they share similar results in regard to routing, maintain their routing tables in very different manners. This results in different solutions when routing problems occur. Match the following items with either RIP (1), OSPF (2), or both (3):**
   a. Silent ______ routers do not transmit route information to other routers.
   b. The Dead interval should be at least four times the Hello interval.
   c. Routers using authentication should use the same password.
   d. It can have a maximum of 15 hops.
   e. All router IDs must be unique.
   f. All neighboring routers must use the same authentication setting (on/off), password, Hello interval, Dead interval, Area ID, and stub setting.
   g. Routing tables should be manually inspected.
2. **Which of the following items should be performed first?**
   a. Reconfigure the update or announcement or each router.
   b. Reinstall the routing protocol.
   c. Verify that hardware connections are functioning properly.
   d. Remove, then rebind all interfaces.
3. **All routers that must communicate with each other must run the same IP routing protocol.**
   a. True
   b. False
4. **Which of the following is a valid action when troubleshooting router problems? (Choose all that apply.)**
   a. Check name resolution processes (DNS and WINS).
   b. Remove, then reinstall, the IP routing protocol.
   c. Check IP configurations, especially gateways, on all affected systems.
   d. Check routing tables with the route print command.
   e. Install all available routing protocols on each router.
   f. Use the pathping command to verify connections between systems.
   g. Use Network Monitor to capture traffic and inspect it for routing data.
   h. Check the router configuration and routing protocol configuration.
   i. Disconnect all systems from the network, then add one system at a time until routing fails.
   j. Double-check update settings, convergence times, and neighbor configurations.
5. **The ROUTETST utility can be used to perform a network-wide routing inspection. It displays all possible routes between the host system and all other systems on the network, as well as any problems it encounters.**
   a. True
   b. False

OBJECTIVES

6.4 Update a Windows 2000-based routing table by means of static routes

STATIC ROUTES • ROUTING TABLES • RIP • OSPF

UNDERSTANDING THE OBJECTIVE

RIP and OSPF are dynamic routing protocols used in complex routing situations. When only a few routers are present, a static routing table can be defined using the route command. You can also add static routes to the dynamic table maintained by RIP or OSPF.

WHAT YOU REALLY NEED TO KNOW

- Windows 2000 has a single router table, no matter how many interfaces or routing protocols are present.
- The route command can be used from the command prompt or Run command.
- The roue command's syntax is: route [-f] [-p] [*command* [*destination*] [mask *subnetmask*] [*gateway*] [metric *costmetric*]]
  - The-f parameter is used to clear the routing table.
  - The-p parameter is used to make a route persistent across reboots.
  - The *command* option should be replaced with print, add, delete, or change.
  - The *destination* option should be replaced with a host IP address, subnet address, network address, or default gateway address.
  - The mask option defines what portion of the destination address must match in order for the route to be used.
  - The *gateway* option should be replaced with the IP address where the traffic should be directed.
  - The metric option is used to define a hop cost to the route with *costmetric* (an integer).
- To view a list of the current routing table, issue the route print command from a command prompt.
- New static routes can also be created through the Routing and Remote Access utility by issuing the New Static Route command when the Static Route folder is selected.

OBJECTIVES ON THE JOB

Static routes can often be used to temporarily redirect traffic around a failed or congested network segment. They can also be used to permanently redirect traffic through a preferred route or link. The route command is useful when performing remote instructions on Telnet-controlled routers or local Windows 2000 Server routing systems. When making numerous changes, use the route command in a batch file. When performing single route changes, the GUI is often easier to use on Windows 2000 Server systems.

PRACTICE TEST QUESTIONS

1. **Which command displays a list of the currently defined routes?**
   a. Route add
   b. Route print
   c. Route delete
   d. Route change
2. **To make a permanent change to the routing table, which parameter should be used with the route command?**
   a. -f
   b. -p
   c. -x
   d. -b
3. **Windows 2000 supports a routing table for each interface and for each routing protocol.**
   a. True
   b. False
4. **There are several optional command elements for the route command:**
   1. command
   2. destination
   3. mask
   4. gateway
   5. metric
   6. costmetric

   Match the following descriptions with one or more of these elements:
   a. Should be replaced with a host IP address, subnet address, network address, or default gateway address
   b. Should be replaced with print, add, delete, and change
   c. Should be replaced with the IP address where the traffic should be redirected
   d. A variable that must be replaced with a specific value
   e. Used to define which portion of the destination address must match in order for the route to be used
   f. A command or identifier which must be followed by a variable
   g. Used to define a hop cost to the route
   h. A route hop cost as an integer
5. **Which of the following statements is true? (Choose all that apply.)**
   a. The GUI is the best location to create multiple static routes.
   b. The route command is the best tool to create multiple static routes.
   c. The GUI can be scripted to execute as a batch file.
   d. The route command can be scripted to execute as a batch file.
   e. Static routes can only be defined when RIP and OSPF are not in use.
   f. Static routes can be defined whether or not RIP and OSPF are not in use.

OBJECTIVES

6.5 Implement Demand-Dial Routing

DEMAND-DIAL ROUTING • DIAL-ON-DEMAND

UNDERSTANDING THE OBJECTIVE

Routes for network traffic are not always permanently cabled connections. Dial-on-demand, or demand-dial routing, is the process of establishing a communication link between the router and another system in order to provide a route over which to direct traffic.

WHAT YOU REALLY NEED TO KNOW

- A Windows 2000 Server router can dial up another Windows 2000 Server router to establish an alternate temporary communication pathway.
- A port must be configured to support demand-dial routing before a demand-dial interface is defined. This is done through the properties of the Ports folder.
- Once defined, a demand-dial route is used only when the router determines it is the best (or only) route to the destination. When this occurs, the system initiates a remote access link, which requires a logon and authentication. After the connection is established, the traffic is routed over the new link.
- A demand-dial route can be initiated via a modem, **ISDN**, or other physical connection device, or over a VPN link.
- A demand-dial route can be defined as an on-demand or persistent connection. The former terminates after a short period of time without any traffic. The latter retains a functioning connection as long as possible and often reconnects if the link is broken. On-demand connections can cause problems for time-sensitive applications due to the delay in re-establishing the communication link.
- Demand-dial routes can be one way or two way. In a one-way configuration, only a single router is configured to dial out and connect to an answering router. In a two-way configuration, both are configured to dial out and answer as needed.

OBJECTIVES ON THE JOB

Demand-dial routing can provide a cost-effective solution for low-traffic, router-to-router connections by providing access only when required. All of the security configurations, restrictions, and concerns related to remote access for clients are the same in relation to routers. Thus, they can be controlled in the same way with remote access policies, profiles, permissions, authentication, encryption, callback, caller ID, dial-out hours, demand-dial filters, and remote access account lockout.

PRACTICE TEST QUESTIONS

1. **FREG Inc. has two large offices, one in New York and another in Los Angeles. Data from both networks is shared over a VPN link. However, the VPN link goes offline often due to Internet traffic jams or ISP issues. Management asked that a backup plan be put into operation, which will provide an alternate communication link in the event of a VPN failure. Which of the following options is the most cost-effective and results in a link only when needed?**
    a. A leased direct fiber-optic link
    b. An on-demand telephone demand-dial route
    c. A line-of-sight microwave bridge
    d. A persistent telephone demand-dial route
2. **After implementing your solution, the VPN link remains up for more than two weeks. However, on a Tuesday afternoon, the VPN goes down. Users in Los Angeles report they are unable to gain access to the New York LAN at times, but the New York users report they don't have problems accessing data from the Los Angeles LAN, except for slow speed. What is the problem?**
    a. A two-way demand-dial route is in use.
    b. A one-way demand-dial route from New York is in use.
    c. A one-way demand-dial route from Los Angeles is in use.
    d. A persistent demand-dial route is in use.
3. **Demand-dial routing is enabled by default when the Network Router option is selected from the Configure and Enable Routing and Remote Access Wizard.**
    a. True
    b. False
4. **Which of the following can be used to restrict or control demand-dial routing? (Choose all that apply.)**
    a. Remote access policies
    b. Remote access profiles
    c. Remote access permissions
    d. Authentication
    e. Encryption
    f. NTFS permissions
    g. Callback
    h. Caller ID
    i. Dial-out hours
5. **A demand dial routing connection is established only after a user's logon credentials are transmitted and verified by the answering router.**
    a. True
    b. False

OBJECTIVES

6.6 Manage and monitor border routing

BORDER ROUTING • ABR • LSDB • ASBR

UNDERSTANDING THE OBJECTIVE

Border routing and internal routing are designations that have meaning only with the OSPF IP routing protocol. Border routing management is mostly an understanding of your internal/external routes and proper configuration of your routing systems.

WHAT YOU REALLY NEED TO KNOW

- An OSPF-routed network has at least one area labeled as the backbone. This is true even if the network is not subdivided into areas. The backbone has a reserved area ID of 0.0.0.0, or area 0.
- The backbone functions as a hub of traffic crossing from one area to another. For example, traffic from area 1 must pass through area 0 to reach area 2.
- Backbone routers advertise summary routes for all areas to other areas. For example, area 1' s summary is sent to areas 2 and 3, and area 2's summary is sent to areas 1 and 3, and so on.
- A backbone router is a router with at least one interface in area 0. This can include both ABRs and internal routers.
- An **ABR** is a router with two or more interfaces in different areas. An ABR hosts a unique **LSDB** for each unique area.
- An **ASBR** has at least one interface with an external area (an area not within the local network). It exchanges routing information with external routers. It also advertises external routes to all internal routers, ABRs and backbone routers.
- An external route is any route not contained within an OSPF **AS** (a self-contained routed network). These can include routes from other routing protocols (RIP, **EGP**, **BGP**, and so on), static routes, and routes defined through SNMP.
- External routes can be filtered. Route filters are defined on the External Routing tab of OSPF Properties. A filter basically accepts or denies a path within a specific range (defined with an IP address and subnet mask).

OBJECTIVES ON THE JOB

Managing external, boundary, or border routing is simply a matter of verifying routing tables, interfaces, and configuration settings. Router management needs to take place on a regular basis. The more complex your network's configuration, the more often you need to verify that routing is working properly.

PRACTICE TEST QUESTIONS

1. **How is a backbone router defined?**
   a. The Enable autonomous system boundary router option is checked.
   b. It has at least two interfaces in different areas.
   c. It is configured to accept routing information from external sources.
   d. It has an area label of 0.0.0.0.
2. **Which of the following statements is true? (Choose all that apply.)**
   a. Data on a network is routed through the backbone area when traveling from one area to another.
   b. A backbone router has an area definition of 1.
   c. Backbone routers advertise summary routes for each area.
   d. An ABR is a router with two or more interfaces in different areas.
   e. An ABR hosts a unique LSDB for each unique area.
   f. An ASBR has at least one interface with an external area.
   g. An ASBR exchanges routing information with external routers.
   h. An ASBR does not advertise external routes to internal routers, ABRs, or backbone routers.
3. **Which type of router can be a backbone router? (Choose all that apply.)**
   a. ABR
   b. A router using only RIP
   c. Internal routers
   d. ASBR
4. **Backbone routers can contain which type of routing information? (Choose all that apply.)**
   a. Area summaries
   b. Internal routing tables
   c. External routing tables
   d. Static routes
   e. Routes defined through SNMP
5. **Routes defined by non-OSPF routing protocols are known as ______.**
   a. inter-area routes
   b. external routes
   c. OSPF-plus routes
   d. Microsoft extended routes
6. **Which of the following can be used to prevent external routes from being propagated throughout an autonomous system? (Choose all that apply.)**
   a. Use only internal routing.
   b. Disable ASBR on all backbone routers.
   c. Use Silent RIP.
   d. Use route filters.

OBJECTIVES

6.7 Manage and monitor internal routing

BORDER ROUTING • INTERNAL ROUTING

UNDERSTANDING THE OBJECTIVE

Border routing and internal routing are designations that have meaning only with the OSPF IP routing protocol. Internal routing is used when no communication with external routes is required. External routes include non-OSPF routing protocol routes, static routes, or SNMP defined routes. This objective may also refer to generalized routing oversight as well.

WHAT YOU REALLY NEED TO KNOW

- Internal routing is a mechanism used to limit the routing tables (and therefore, routing pathways) of OSPF routers to only internal systems.
- Internal routing is subdivided by assigning an area ID on OSPF interfaces.
- An internal router has only a single database of routes, known as an LSDB.
- Internal routing does not use summaries of other OSPF-managed areas: instead each router has a full path to every network area. This allows the router to provide the least-cost path to the destination.
- Internal routing has all routers configured not to use external routing (the Enable autonomous system boundary router is not set).
- In general, once RIP or OSPF is installed, it manages routing on its own. More specifically, the routing protocol manages the routes used to move data around the network.
- At any time, you can view the following statistics associated with routing through the Routing and Remote Access utility:
  - TCP/IP information
  - Multicast forwarding table
  - Multicast statistics
  - Current routing table
- Some of the same statistical data can be seen by issuing the route print command from a command prompt.

OBJECTIVES ON THE JOB

Managing internal routing is simply a matter of verifying routing tables, interfaces, and configuration settings. Router management needs to take place on a regular basis. The more complex your network's configuration, the more often you need to verify that routing is working properly.

PRACTICE TEST QUESTIONS

1. **Which of the following statements is true? (Choose all that apply.)**
   a. Internal routing is a function or label used within OSPF routed networks.
   b. Internal routing is used when no communication with external networks is required.
   c. Assigning an area ID on OSPF interfaces is only used in regard to internal routing.
   d. Internal routing does not include or use non-OSPF routing protocol routes, static routes, or SNMP defined routes.
   e. Internal routing is a mechanism used to limit the routing tables (and therefore, routing pathways) of OSPF routers to only internal systems.
   f. Each internal router maintains a unique LSDB for each interface.
2. **When internal routing is used, each router maintains a complete path to all other areas in the network.**
   a. True
   b. False
3. **Which routing states or implementations employ a least-cost path to the destination evaluation when determining which route to use for transmitting data? (Choose all that apply.)**
   a. Internal routing
   b. Border routing
   c. RIP routing
   d. OSPF routing
4. **Internal routing is used when no external routing interfaces are defined or enabled.**
   a. True
   b. False
5. **When internal routing is used, the only means of sending traffic to external systems is a default gateway.**
   a. True
   b. False

OBJECTIVES

6.8 Manage and monitor IP routing protocols

IP ROUTING PROTOCOLS • NETWORK MONITOR

UNDERSTANDING THE OBJECTIVE

Managing and monitoring IP routing are tasks that closely intertwined with maintaining a functioning network. Although routing under Windows 2000 is fairly self-sufficient, maintaining oversight of the operation may help locate and resolve potential problems or catch new problems before they affect the entire network.

WHAT YOU REALLY NEED TO KNOW

- One part of managing IP routing is being prepared to perform troubleshooting when necessary.
- Managing IP routing also involves the use of static routes when necessary. Static routes can be used to temporarily or permanently reroute network traffic around a damaged, overloaded, or restricted network area or toward a preferred or high-speed network area.
- Network Monitor is an excellent tool for watching routed traffic. It can be used to capture inbound and outbound network packets from your router server. Captured packets can be inspected to discover source addresses, destination addresses, protocol headers, and more.
- IP routing can be managed remotely. To do this, add a server to the Routing and Remote Access utility. Once the remote server is listed, you can perform the same management and configuration operations as you do for local systems.
- When monitoring routing, regularly check the following items:
  - Verify that all routing interfaces are active. If any interfaces are found to be inactive, attempt to reset or repair the problem. This can result in the deletion and re-creation (and subsequent reconfiguration) of an interface.
  - Check the routing table on each router. If discrepancies are found, consider deleting the individual entries, defining new entries, or clearing the entire table.
  - Check the status of the Routing and Remote Access service itself. If it is not active, try to restart the service through the Services utility or the Routing and Remote Access utility. If that fails, check Event Viewer's logs for possible error details. Problems that prevent the services from executing may be resolved with a system reboot, but they may be serious enough to warrant a reinstallation of the Windows 2000 operating system.

OBJECTIVES ON THE JOB

Management and monitoring are tedious manual tasks that must be performed on a regular basis. In most cases, failing to watch over your systems results in more serious problems (ones that stop network functionality rather than just interrupt or delay it). Proper vigilance in monitoring often prevents the need for emergency troubleshooting.

PRACTICE TEST QUESTIONS

1. **Which of the following is a common or typical activity in managing routing? (Choose all that apply.)**
   a. Troubleshooting
   b. Monitoring network traffic
   c. Monitoring DHCP
   d. Configuring router interfaces
   e. Verifying router tables
   f. Reviewing the Event Viewer logs
   g. Stopping and restarting the DNS service
2. **Network Monitor can be used to ______. (Choose all that apply.)**
   a. capture traffic inbound to a router server
   b. capture traffic outbound from a router server
   c. inspect the destination and source addresses of network traffic
   d. adjust the router table on a router server
   e. test for optimal use of router pathways
3. **Use of static routes can serve as an element of router and route management.**
   a. True
   b. False
4. **The Routing and Remote Access utility can be used to ______. (Choose all that apply.)**
   a. define static routes
   b. view routing tables
   c. manage router servers located elsewhere on the network
   d. block routed traffic based on a user account
   e. install IP routing protocols
   f. define routing interfaces
   g. configure boundary routing
   h. review Event Viewer for routing related details.
   i. clear the routing table.

Section 7

Installing, Configuring, and Troubleshooting Network Address Translation (NAT)

OBJECTIVES

7.1 Install Internet Connection Sharing

INTERNET CONNECTION SHARING

UNDERSTANDING THE OBJECTIVE

Internet Connection Sharing is a Windows 2000 service that allows clients on a small network to share a single dial-up connection.

WHAT YOU REALLY NEED TO KNOW

- ◆ Internet Connection Sharing can be installed on a network of any size, but it is designed for smaller networks (fewer than 10 clients).
- ◆ Internet Connection Sharing can be enabled on any Windows 2000 system that has a defined Internet connection object (usually with a modem or other dial-up connection device).
- ◆ By default, once Internet Connection Sharing is enabled, the connection is also configured as a demand-dial router. This means that any client on the network can request access to the Internet and a new connection will be established if one is not already live.
- ◆ Internet Connection Sharing is created through combining several services:
  - NAT: The local network connection is assigned an IP address of 192.168.0.1 with a subnet mask of 255.255.255.0.
  - AutoDHCP: A limited version of DHCP is installed to automatically configure clients to participate in the 192.168.0.0 network. (They must be set to obtain an IP address automatically.)
  - DNS proxy: Used to forward DNS queries to the DNS server defined on the Internet connection interface (defined by the ISP).
- ◆ The address 192.168.0.1 is a public address. Public IP addresses are defined in RFC 1918. Public IP addresses are not forwarded by routers by default.
- ◆ The Settings button on the Sharing tab can be used to define additional applications (outbound) or services (inbound) for use over the Internet link. Outbound applications of **FTP**, **ICMP**, SMTP, POP, Web, and Telnet are enabled by default. Inbound services of FTP, ICMP, SMTP, POP, Web, and Telnet are defined but not enabled. Other custom applications and services can be added, but knowledge of the TCP and UDP ports used is required.
- ◆ Internet Connection Sharing cannot be used on networks where DHCP is already present. Also, it is not recommended to deploy Internet Connection Sharing on networks with DNS servers.

OBJECTIVES ON THE JOB

Internet Connection Sharing should only be used on small networks (less than 10 clients). Routing and Remote Access can be used in Network Router mode to share a high-speed dedicated connection with a large network.

PRACTICE TEST QUESTIONS

1. **Internet Connection Sharing includes elements of which of the following services or features of Windows 2000? (Choose all that apply.)**
   a. DHCP
   b. WINS
   c. DNS
   d. Telnet
   e. NAT
   f. SNMP
2. **Which of the following resources cannot be accessed over an Internet Connection Sharing link by default? (Choose all that apply.)**
   a. Web
   b. FTP
   c. IRC
   d. Telnet
   e. E-mail
   f. Windows streaming media
3. **Internet Connection Sharing can only be used on Windows 2000 Professional systems.**
   a. True
   b. False
4. **Internet Connection Sharing is a realistic option in which of the following situations? (Choose all that apply.)**
   a. Enterprise networks
   b. Small office/home office networks
   c. Networks already using DHCP
   d. Networks with a single Windows 2000 Professional client and five Windows 98 clients
5. **What changes are made to the Local Area Connection on the Windows 2000 system hosting Internet Connection Sharing?**
   a. It is configured to use DHCP.
   b. It is configured to obtain its IP configuration automatically.
   c. It is configured to use a static public IP address.
   d. It is configured as a WINS proxy.
   e. It is not altered in any way.
6. **Which of the following statements is true? (Choose all that apply.)**
   a. Internet Connection Sharing objects are configured by default as demand-dial routers.
   b. Internet Connection Sharing can be used on LAN Internet connections.
   c. Internet Connection Sharing does not allow Internet users to connect to internal Web sites.
   d. Internet Connection Sharing enables clients to use an ISP's DNS servers.

OBJECTIVES

7.2 Install NAT

NAT INSTALLATION

UNDERSTANDING THE OBJECTIVE

NAT is probably the best feature of Windows 2000 for networks requiring Internet access. NAT enables a high-bandwidth connection to be securely and economically shared by clients within the entire network.

WHAT YOU REALLY NEED TO KNOW

- NAT is installed through the Routing and Remote Access utility.
- NAT should be used on networks where Internet Connection Sharing is not adequate. This usually means that either the network has 10 or more clients, or that greater Internet connection bandwidth is needed.
- Routing and Remote Access must be configured as a network router or an Internet router in order for NAT to be used to grant Internet access to network clients.
- NAT offers the ability to share one or a few leased IP addresses for direct Internet access with numerous clients. This is done by proxying Internet resource access for the clients.
- NAT, used through Routing and Remote Access, does not cache Internet content. It simply acts as a mediator between the client and the Internet.
- NAT functions by replacing the source address (the client) with its own address on all traffic outbound to the Internet. It maintains a mapping between the source address (Internet server) and the client so it can direct the response to the appropriate client.
- NAT offers two benefits:
  1. Security. NAT effectively hides the internal structure of the network from the Internet.
  2. Reduced costs. A network can use the private IP addresses (defined in RFC 1918) instead of leasing an address for each client.

OBJECTIVES ON THE JOB

With NAT, networks can share high-bandwidth connections simply and easily. NAT prevents external origination of communications, thereby virtually eliminating external attacks. NAT can be used between any two interfaces, including other LANs, WANs, and Internet links.

PRACTICE TEST QUESTIONS

1. **FOOLL Inc. has recently deployed several Windows 2000 Server systems and upgraded some clients to Windows 2000 Professional. Other systems on the network include Windows NT and Windows 98. The network needs Internet access, so the company contracted with an ISP to obtain a dedicated 256 MB fiber-optic link. Which of the following additional configuration options results in the most cost-effective solution? (Choose all that apply.)**
   a. Lease an IP address for each system on the network.
   b. Deploy Routing and Remote Access on a Windows 2000 Server system as a network router and connect the high-speed Internet link to this system.
   c. Deploy a modem on each system, with a dedicated phone line, and have each system establish a dial-up connection to the Windows 2000 Server system.
   d. Deploy NAT and use private IP addresses for all internal systems on the network.
2. **After deploying your preferred solution, FOOLL Inc. decides to hire an additional 50 employees to add to its existing 125. Each employee has a desktop workstation that must have Internet access. What additional configuration settings, other than a client configuration, are needed to support these new clients?**
   a. Lease additional IP addresses.
   b. Deploy a second Windows 2000 Server system with Routing and Remote Access.
   c. Define additional access ports on the network router.
   d. None
3. **NAT cannot be used on networks employing DHCP.**
   a. True
   b. False
4. **Which of the following is a benefit of NAT? (Choose all that apply.)**
   a. Security
   b. Traffic monitoring
   c. Low cost
   d. Router management
5. **NAT is installed as a ______.**
   a. network service
   b. network protocol
   c. routing protocol
   d. network client
6. **NAT can be used on which of the following? (Choose all that apply.)**
   a. Enterprise networks
   b. Small office/home office networks
   c. Networks requiring at least 64 KB of bandwidth per client
   d. Networks on which IRC is required

OBJECTIVES

7.3 Configure NAT properties

NAT • SYSTEM LOG

UNDERSTANDING THE OBJECTIVE

The default configuration of NAT supports most network needs. However, you can modify several properties to fine-tune NAT to your specific network and Internet requirements.

WHAT YOU REALLY NEED TO KNOW

- NAT is configured through its own properties dialog box, accessed through the Routing and Remote Access utility.
- NAT can record data about its activity to the System Log viewed through Event Viewer. The log settings include log errors only (default), log errors and warnings, log the maximum amount of information, or disable event logging.
- NAT's primary function is to mediate communications between internal clients and external services through the installation of IP addresses.
- IP address mappings are maintained in memory for a specified time period. These settings can be changed from the default of 1440 minutes for TCP mappings to one minute for UDP mappings.
- NAT includes a limited version of DHCP, as does Internet Connection Sharing. This feature is disabled by default. This allows NAT to be used on networks already employing DHCP.
- When DHCP is enabled through NAT, it assigns IP addresses to clients in a specific range. The default range is 192.168.0.0, with a subnet mask of 255.255.255.0. You can define address exclusions for addresses that are statically assigned or that are being used for some other purpose.
- If name resolution is needed, NAT can be configured to forward DNS queries. DNS query management is disabled by default. When enabled, queries are forwarded to the router's configured DNS server or to the public Internet for resolution. You can choose to dial an Internet connection when a query must be resolved.

OBJECTIVES ON THE JOB

Unless you are experiencing a problem with NAT, record only errors or disable logging completely. Otherwise, your System Log quickly fills up with event details you don't need. It's also important to properly configure the DHCP service of NAT, if you decide to employ it. Be sure to define a network range that includes your own Local Area Connection's IP configuration—then be sure to exclude it from being assigned to some other client.

PRACTICE TEST QUESTIONS

1. **Which of the following statements is true?**
   a. NAT must be configured before it will support network activity.
   b. NAT's timeouts are inconsistent with normal network/Internet activity.
   c. NAT requires LMHOSTS files on each client.
   d. NAT's default configuration will work in most cases.
2. **NAT's primary purpose is to ______.**
   a. cache Internet content for faster retrieval by network clients
   b. mediate communications between internal clients and external services through translation of IP addresses
   c. route network traffic from one subnet to another
   d. filter network traffic based on application, IP address, protocol, or user
3. **NAT is functional immediately after installation.**
   a. True
   b. False
4. **What timeouts can be configured for NAT? (Choose all that apply.)**
   a. DHCP IP lease duration
   b. UDP mapping duration
   c. Response from server timeout
   d. TCP mapping duration
5. **NAT can handle domain name resolution queries in which of the following ways? (Choose all that apply.)**
   a. Forward to locally defined DNS servers
   b. Forward to Internet DNS servers
   c. Forward to WINS servers
   d. Forward to DHCP servers
6. **Which of the following are valid configuration options for NAT? (Choose all that apply.)**
   a. Log only errors
   b. Restrict access based on group membership
   c. Set the TCP mapping timeout in minutes
   d. Define additional applications to be supported over the link
   e. Import HOSTS files
   f. Use DHCP to assign client IP addresses
   g. Load balance traffic over multilink Internet connections
   h. Define exclusions to prevent specific IP addresses from being assigned to clients
   i. Restrict bandwidth usage by subnet
   j. Forward DNS queries
   k. Establish a dial-out connection to the Internet to handle domain name queries
   l. Record all network packets to a storage device

OBJECTIVES

7.4 Troubleshoot NAT interfaces

NAT • INTERFACE

UNDERSTANDING THE OBJECTIVE

NAT troubleshooting is frequently a process of ensuring network communications and redefining the interfaces. NAT usually functions without management or need of troubleshooting. When problems occur, 99 percent of the time they are network communication-related (such as broken links, bottlenecks, dropped packets, and so on) rather than NAT-related.

WHAT YOU REALLY NEED TO KNOW

- Once NAT is installed, you must define interfaces that use NAT. At least two interfaces (one for the internal network, the other for the external network) are required for NAT to function. The external network is usually the Internet.
- The internal network connection must be configured as a private interface connected to a private network. No other configuration occurs on this interface.
- The external network connection must be configured as a public interface connected to the Internet. You should also select the Translate TCP/UDP headers option to allow other computers to transmit data over this interface, define all of the addresses assigned to you by the ISP, and define any unique or custom port designations required by applications or services on your network.
- When NAT doesn't function as expected, try the following:
  1. Check network connections with the ping, pathping, and tracert commands.
  2. Check that at least two interfaces (one public and one private) for NAT are defined.
  3. Stop and restart the Routing and Remote Access service.
  4. Reboot the Routing and Remote Access host system.
  5. Delete and re-create NAT interfaces.
  6. Remove and reinstall the NAT routing protocol.

OBJECTIVES ON THE JOB

NAT is a self-sufficient service of the Windows 2000 Routing and Remote Access utility. In the rare event of a failure, attempt to verify network communications before reconfiguring NAT. Only delete interfaces or remove the NAT protocol as a last resort. Problems rarely arise that require that level of action.

PRACTICE TEST QUESTIONS

1. **How many interfaces are required by NAT?**
   a. one
   b. two
   c. three
   d. four

2. **What types of interfaces are required by NAT? (Choose all that apply.)**
   a. Public
   b. Private
   c. Multihomed
   d. Integrated

3. **Through what interface type does NAT offer additional configuration options?**
   a. Public
   b. Private
   c. Multihomed
   d. Integrated

4. **Which of the following are valid troubleshooting steps when attempting to resolve a problem associated with NAT? (Choose all that apply.)**
   a. Check network connections using the ping, pathping, and tracert commands.
   b. Capture traffic with Network Monitor and look for ICMP packets.
   c. Check that at least two interfaces (one public and one private) for NAT are defined.
   d. Use System Monitor to track total bandwidth consumption over the Network Segment object.
   e. Stop and restart the Routing and Remote Access service.
   f. Reinstall Windows 2000.
   g. Reboot the Routing and Remote Access host system.
   h. Delete and re-create NAT interfaces.
   i. Remove the Network Monitor Agent driver.
   j. Remove and reinstall the NAT routing protocol.
   k. Stop the Spooler service.

5. **The translation of TCP/UDP headers on a public interface allows all of the computers within a network to communicate with the Internet through NAT.**
   a. True
   b. False

6. **If you need to define special communications channels needed by applications or services on your network so they will function properly over NAT, what configuration tab do you need?**
   a. General
   b. Address Pool
   c. Special Ports
   d. Applications and Services

Section 8

Installing, Configuring, Managing, Monitoring, and Troubleshooting Certificate Services

OBJECTIVES

8.1 Install and configure Certificate Authority

CA • ENTERPRISE • STANDALONE

UNDERSTANDING THE OBJECTIVE

Windows 2000 Server can be a CA simply by installing Certificate Services. Certificate Services can be used to issue, renew, verify, and revoke certificates for users, servers, and other CAs.

WHAT YOU REALLY NEED TO KNOW

- Certificate Services can be installed during initial installation (whether manual or scripted) of Windows 2000 Server, or anytime afterward through the Windows Components section of the Add/Remove Programs utility.
- When a **CA** is installed, it can be one of four types:
  - Enterprise Root CA: one per enterprise, requires Active Directory, must be a parent, and acts as the root CA of an enterprise
  - Enterprise Subordinate CA: requires Active Directory, obtains its certificate from a parent CA, is a child of another CA, and can be a parent to other CAs
  - Standalone Root CA: Active Directory is not required and is usually positioned offline to provide a safe storage location for original certificates and encryption keys
  - Standalone Subordinate CA: Active Directory is not required, obtains its certificate from a parent CA, is a child of another CA, and can be a parent to other CAs
- Once Certificate Services is installed, the system cannot be renamed nor can it join or leave a domain.
- A root CA must be installed first. Then subordinate CAs can be installed.
- During installation, you will need to make the following configuration choices:
  - Type of CA to install (enterprise/standalone and root/subordinate)
  - Whether to use advanced options:
    - Select a cryptographic service provider (CSP)
    - Select a hash algorithm
    - Whether to use existing keys
    - Key length
  - CA name, organization name, **OU**, locality (city), state/province, country (x.500 two-character code), path location of database and log, and shared folder
  - Where to request CA certificate for an enterprise CA, either from a parent CA or an offline source (save to a file for manual transmission)

OBJECTIVES ON THE JOB

Installing and configuring Certificate Services to establish CAs on your network is performed in a single, multistep activity. Once installation is complete, the CA is ready to perform certificate management activities.

PRACTICE TEST QUESTIONS

1. **Match these four types of CAs with their descriptions:**
    1. Enterprise Root CA
    2. Enterprise Subordinate CA
    3. Standalone Root CA
    4. Standalone Subordinate CA

    a. Requires Active Directory, obtains its certificate from a parent CA, is a child of another CA, and can be a parent to other CAs
    b. Active Directory is not required, obtains its certificate from a parent CA, is a child of another CA, and can be a parent to other CAs
    c. One per enterprise, requires Active Directory, must be a parent, and acts as the root CA of an enterprise
    d. Active Directory is not required and is usually positioned offline to provide a safe storage location for original certificates and encryption keys
2. **Certificate Services can be installed on Windows 2000 Server through what means? (Choose all that apply.)**
    a. Through the Add/Remove Programs applet after Windows 2000 Server is already installed
    b. Through IntelliMirror
    c. During initial installation by manually selecting a service
    d. During an automated initial installation using an unattend.txt file
3. **Windows 2000 Server systems with Certificate Services installed can have their host names changed so they can alter their domain membership.**
    a. True
    b. False
4. **Which of the following is a type of credential or data item that must be provided when configuring a CA? (Choose all that apply.)**
    a. Organization name
    b. Domain name
    c. CA name
    d. Administrator account name
    e. OU
    f. Locality
    g. IP address
    h. State/province
    i. WINS server address
    j. Country
    k. Security password
5. **When a CA is being installed as a standalone CA, which of the following configuration options do not appear or are requested?**
    a. Whether to use advanced options
    b. Path locations for the database and log
    c. Where to request CA certificate for this CA
    d. Name of the shared folder

OBJECTIVES

8.2 Issue and revoke certificates

CA • CRL • IIS • ACTIVE DIRECTORY

UNDERSTANDING THE OBJECTIVE

Certificate management is simple through Certificate Services on Windows 2000.

WHAT YOU REALLY NEED TO KNOW

- CAs issue certificates only after a request for a certificate has been made. A request for a certificate can originate from a user, a computer, a service, or other CAs.
- Certificates are managed through the Certificate Services snap-in of the MMC.
- Users can manage their own certificates; administrators can manage certificates for their assigned OU.
- Through the Certificate console, you can request a certification from any CA available on the network.
- Certificates can also be requested through *http://Caservername/certsvr/*. This site is created automatically on systems where IIS is present when Certificate Server is installed. You can also view the status of certificate requests through this Web site.
- Certificate requests are processed immediately upon receipt. This results in either a failed or granted status on enterprise CAs, but on standalone CAs the request is marked as pending.
- Certificate mapping is a mechanism by which a user account uses a certificate to log on to the network, rather than a user name and password. Mapping can occur through Active Directory or IIS.
- One-to-one mapping is a single user account mapped to a single certificate. Many-to-one mapping is when a single user account has many certificates from different CAs mapped to it.
- Specific certificates can be revoked by highlighting the certificate and issuing the Revoke command.
- Once a certificate is revoked, it is added to the **CRL**. The CRL is periodically distributed among the network CAs. This ensures that a revoked certificate is not used to gain access.

OBJECTIVES ON THE JOB

Be sure to carefully plan out the structure of your CAs. Keep track of active certificates so only those users who should have access at any given moment actually have live certificates. Many-to-one mapping may be useful when two or more large networks are combined, and resources from both connected networks are required by each user.

PRACTICE TEST QUESTIONS

1. **Certificates can be issued to ______. (Choose all that apply.)**
   a. computers
   b. domains
   c. services
   d. non-Windows 2000 systems
   e. CAs
   f. groups
   g. users
   h. OUs
2. **When a certificate request is received by a standalone CA, what status level can that request be granted automatically?**
   a. Revoked
   b. Issued
   c. Pending
   d. Failed
3. **Through what means can a certificate request be sent to a CA? (Choose all that apply.)**
   a. Over an intranet link to a Web site
   b. From the System applet
   c. Through the Network and Dial-up Connections utility
   d. Through an MMC
4. **Which of the following is a valid option offered to you when revoking a certificate? (Choose all that apply.)**
   a. Restriction of remote access
   b. Unspecified
   c. Key compromise
   d. Locked-out account
   e. CA compromise
   f. Change of affiliation
   g. Routing limitation
   h. Temporary leave of absence
5. **When a certificate is revoked, it is added to the ______, which is regularly distributed among the CAs to ensure that a revoked certificate is not used.**
   a. CRT
   b. CRL
   c. NAT
   d. CAX

OBJECTIVES

8.3 Remove the EFS recovery keys

EFS RECOVERY KEY REMOVAL

UNDERSTANDING THE OBJECTIVE

NTFS's EFS security feature is based on an encryption key. This key is stored locally on the hard drive by default. This is an insecure configuration.

WHAT YOU REALLY NEED TO KNOW

- After configuration, the **EFS** encryption key should be exported and stored on removable media or a network share, and then removed from the system's hard drive.
- You export the EFS encryption key via the Certificate Services snap-in for the MMC.
- The exported key should be protected. Thus, if this is removable media, it should be locked up when not in use.
- This key is required each time you wish to access encrypted data.
- To import the encryption key, issue the Import command from the Action menu. You must provide the path to the key file, the password to unlock the key file, and where in the certificate store to save the key (automatic or in a specific location).

OBJECTIVES ON THE JOB

EFS is effective as long as the encryption key is not accessible to unauthorized users. It is easy to extract data directly from a hard drive, even from NTFS volumes. If the encryption key is on the hard drive, it can be used to decrypt EFS-protected files. The only way EFS provides meaningful protection is if you keep the key stored in a secure location.

PRACTICE TEST QUESTIONS

1. **EFS is a feature of ______.**
    a. DNS
    b. NTFS
    c. Certificate Services
    d. dynamic storage

2. **Where is the EFS encryption key stored by default?**
    a. On a floppy
    b. In the Registry
    c. In a file on the hard drive
    d. In Active Directory

3. **If a hard drive is compromised and an NTFS reader is used, a hacker can easily extract encrypted data from the drive if the encryption key has not been exported and deleted.**
    a. True
    b. False

4. **What is the only way for EFS to provide true protection?**
    a. Use strong encryption.
    b. Use NTFS on all partitions.
    c. Use Active Directory.
    d. Remove the EFS key from the system.

5. **When an EFS key is exported, what additional security feature can be used to protect that key from being imported by someone else?**
    a. Logon authentication
    b. Internal encryption
    c. A timestamp
    d. A password
    e. Group membership
    f. Domain association

6. **After an EFS encryption key has been exported, what must the valid user do in order to access EFS-protected files?**
    a. Provide the unlock password.
    b. Import the key.
    c. Disconnect from the network.
    d. Install Active Directory.
    e. Remove Certificate Services.

7. **When a key is exported, it is always automatically deleted from the base system no matter what configuration options are selected during the export.**
    a. True
    b. False

ANSWER KEY

Section 1.0

Objective 1.1

Practice Questions:

1. c
2. b, c
3. b
4. c
5. b
6. d

Objective 1.2

Practice Questions:

1. b, c
2. b
3. b
4. a, b, c
5. a, c
6. a
7. a, d

Objective 1.3

Practice Questions:

1. c
2. b
3. a
4. a
5. a, b
6. d
7. a, d

Objective 1.4

Practice Questions:

1. b
2. c
3. a
4. b
5. b
6. d

Objective 1.5

Practice Questions:

1. b
2. a, b, c, d
3. a
4. a, b, c
5. d
6. b
7. a, b

Objective 1.6

Practice Questions:

1. b
2. c, d
3. b
4. b
5. a, b
6. d
7. b

Objective 1.7

Practice Questions:

1. b
2. a, d
3. b
4. a, c
5. a, b, c
6. a, b, c
7. a

Objective 1.8

Practice Questions:

1. b
2. b
3. a
4. a - 1, 2, 5, 6; b - 1, 3, 7; c - 1, 4
5. a
6. c

Objective 1.9

Practice Questions:

1. a, c
2. a, d
3. a
4. a
5. a, c
6. b
7. b

Objective 1.10

Practice Questions:

1. b
2. a, b, c, d, f
3. b
4. a, c
5. a, b, d, e, g
6. b
7. a, b, c

Objective 1.11

Practice Questions:

1. a - 6, b - 2, c - 4, d - 1, e - 5, f - 3, g - 7
2. a
3. a
4. a, c, d, f, g, i, j
5. b

Objective 1.12

Practice Questions:

1. c
2. c
3. a, b, d, f
4. a
5. b

Section 2.0

Objective 2.1

Practice Questions:

1. d
2. a
3. b
4. b

Objective 2.2

Practice Questions:

1. a, c, e
2. b
3. a
4. a, b, d
5. a
6. b, c, d
7. b

Objective 2.3

Practice Questions:

1. a, c, f, g
2. a, b, d
3. d
4. a, c, d
5. c
6. a
7. b

Objective 2.4

Practice Questions:

1. c
2. b
3. b, c, e, g
4. d

Objective 2.5

Practice Questions:

1. d
2. b
3. a
4. a, b, c
5. a, b
6. a
7. b

Objective 2.6

Practice Questions:

1. c
2. b
3. b
4. a
5. d
6. a
7. c

Objective 2.7

Practice Questions:

1. c
2. b
3. a
4. d
5. a
6. b
7. a, c, d

Objective 2.8

Practice Questions:

1. a
2. b
3. a
4. a, b
5. d
6. c
7. a

Objective 2.9

Practice Questions:

1. a, c, d
2. b
3. a
4. a, b, c
5. a, c, d, f
6. b
7. a

Section 3.0

Objective 3.1

Practice Questions:

1. b, d
2. a
3. a, b, d
4. a
5. a, b, c, d

Objective 3.2

Practice Questions:

1. d
2. c
3. a
4. a, d
5. a, c, e, f
6. b, c, e
7. b

Objective 3.3

Practice Questions:

1. b
2. a, c
3. a
4. a, b, c, e

Objective 3.4

Practice Questions:

1. a, c
2. b
3. a
4. a, d
5. c, d, e

Objective 3.5

Practice Questions:

1. a
2. d
3. a
4. a, b, c, d, e
5. b

Objective 3.6

Practice Questions:

1. b
2. a, b
3. b
4. b, c, d, e, g

Objective 3.7

Practice Questions:

1. d
2. b
3. b
4. c, d
5. a

Objective 3.8

Practice Questions:

1. d
2. c
3. b
4. a, c, e
5. a

Objective 3.9

Practice Questions:

1. b
2. a, d
3. a
4. c, d
5. c, d, e

Objective 3.10

Practice Questions:

1. b
2. b, c
3. a
4. b
5. c
6. c, d
7. a, c, d

Objective 3.11

Practice Questions:

1. d
2. d
3. b
4. a, b, d
5. a, b, c, d

Section 4.0

Objective 4.1

Practice Questions:

1. a, b, c
2. d
3. b
4. a, e, g
5. a, b
6. b, d
7. a, c

Objective 4.2

Practice Questions:

1. d
2. c
3. a
4. a, c, d, e

Objective 4.3

Practice Questions:

1. c
2. a
3. a
4. c, d, e, f
5. a
6. a

Objective 4.4

Practice Questions:

1. b, c, f
2. a, b
3. b
4. a
5. b, c

Objective 4.5

Practice Questions:

1. d
2. c
3. b
4. a, c, d
5. a, b, d
6. b

Objective 4.6

Practice Questions:

1. d
2. b, c
3. a
4. b
5. a, c, d, e
6. a, b, c, d
7. c

Objective 4.7

Practice Questions:

1. c
2. a, b
3. b
4. a, d
5. a, b, c, d

Objective 4.8

Practice Questions:

1. b
2. a, b, c
3. a
4. b, d
5. b
6. b
7. d

Objective 4.9

Practice Questions:

1. d
2. a, c, d
3. a
4. a, b, d, f, g

Objective 4.10

Practice Questions:

1. b
2. b, f, g
3. a
4. b, c, d

Objective 4.11

Practice Questions:

1. a, b
2. c
3. a, c, e
4. a, c
5. a
6. a, b

Objective 4.12

Practice Questions:

1. c, d
2. b
3. a
4. a
5. b
6. a

Section 5.0

Objective 5.1

Practice Questions:

1. c
2. d
3. b
4. b, c, d
5. c

Objective 5.2

Practice Questions:

1. b
2. c
3. a
4. a
5. a, b, d
6. a
7. a

Objective 5.3

Practice Questions:

1. b
2. d
3. b
4. e, b, g, c, f, a, d
5. a
6. c
7. b, d

Objective 5.4

Practice Questions:

1. a, c, e, g
2. c
3. a
4. a, c
5. d
6. b

Objective 5.5

Practice Questions:

1. c
2. b
3. a, d
4. a, b, c, d, e, f, g
5. b

Section 6.0

Objective 6.1

Practice Questions:

1. d
2. a, b
3. a
4. a, d, e
5. a, b, d, e

Objective 6.2

Practice Questions:

1. 1 - a, b ,c; 2 - b, d, e; 3 - c, f, g; 4 - a, h, i
2. b, d, e, f
3. a, b, d
4. b, c, d, f
5. a

Objective 6.3

Practice Questions:

1. 1 – a, d; 2 - b, f, e; 3 - c, g
2. c
3. a
4. a, c, d, f, g, h, j
5. b

Objective 6.4

Practice Questions:

1. b
2. b
3. b
4. 1 - b, d; 2 - a, d; 3 - e, f; 4 - c, d; 5 - f, g; 6 - d, h
5. b, d, f

Objective 6.5

Practice Questions:

1. b
2. b
3. b
4. a, b, c, d, e, g, h, i
5. a

Objective 6.6

Practice Questions:

1. d
2. a, c, d, e, f, g
3. a, c
4. a, b, c, d, e
5. b
6. a, d

Objective 6.7

Practice Questions:

1. a, b, d, e
2. a
3. a, b, d
4. a
5. b

Objective 6.8

Practice Questions:

1. a, b, d, e, f
2. a, b, c
3. a
4. a, b, c, e, f, g

Section 7.0

Objective 7.1

Practice Questions:

1. a, c, e
2. c, f
3. b
4. b, d
5. c
6. a, d

Objective 7.2

Practice Questions:

1. b, d
2. d
3. b
4. a, c
5. c
6. a, b, c, d

Objective 7.3

Practice Questions:

1. d
2. b
3. a
4. b, d
5. a, b
6. a, c, d, f, h, j, k

Objective 7.4

Practice Questions:

1. b
2. a, b
3. a
4. a, c, e, g, h, j
5. a
6. c

Section 8.0

Objective 8.1

Practice Questions:

1. 1 - c, 2 - b, 3 - d, 4 - a
2. a, c, d
3. b
4. a, c, e, f, h, j
5. c

Objective 8.2

Practice Questions:

1. a, c, d, e, g
2. c
3. a, d
4. b, c, e, f
5. b

Objective 8.3

Practice Questions:

1. b
2. c
3. a
4. d
5. d
6. b
7. b

GLOSSARY OF ACRONYMS AND ABBREVIATIONS

A

ABR – area border router
AD – Active Directory
API – Application Programming Interface
AS – autonomous system
ASBR – autonomous system boundary router

B

BAP – Bandwidth Allocation Protocol
BGP – Border Gateway Protocol
BIND – Berkeley Internet Name Domain

C

CA – Certificate of Authority
CHAP – Challenge Handshake Authentication Protocol
CRL – Certificate Revocation List

D

DES – Data Encryption Standard
DHCP – Dynamic Host Configuration Protocol
DNS – Domain Name System
DNSCMD – DNS Command utility
DUN – Dial-up Networking

E

EAP – Extensible Authentication Protocol
EFS – Encrypting File System
EGP – Exterior Gateway Protocol

F

FQDN – fully qualified domain name
FTP – File Transfer Protocol

G

GUI – graphical user interface

I

IAS – Internet Authentication Service
ICMP – Internet Control Message Protocol
ICS – Internet Connection Sharing
IKE – Internet Key Exchange
IP – Internet Protocol
IPCONFIG – IP Configuration
IPSec – Internet Protocol Security
IPX – Internetwork Packet Exchange
IPX/SPX – Internetwork Packet Exchange/Sequenced Packet Exchange
ISDN – Integrated Services Digital Network
ISP – Internet Service Provider

K

KDC – Key Distribution Center

L

L2TP – Layer 2 Tunneling Protocol
LAN – local area network
LSDB – link-state database

M

MAC – Media Access Control
MADCAP – Multicast Address Dynamic Client Allocation Protocol
MMC – Microsoft Management Console
MPPE – Microsoft Point-to-Point Encryption
MS-CHAP – Microsoft Challenge Handshake Authentication Protocol

N

NAT – Network Address Translation
NBMA – Nonbroadcast Multiple Access
NetBEUI – NetBIOS Extended User Interface
NetBIOS – Network Basic Input/Output System
NSLOOKUP – Name Server Lookup
NWLink – NetWare Link

O

OSPF – Open Shortest Path First
OU – Organizational Unit

P

PAP – Password Authentication Protocol
POP3 – Post Office Protocol 3
PPP – Point-to-Point Protocol
PPTP – Point-to-Point Tunneling Protocol

R

RADIUS – Remote Authentication Dial-in User Service
RAM – Random Access Memory
RAS – Remote Access Service
RIP – Routing Information Protocol

S

SLIP – Serial Line Internet Protocol
SMS – Systems Management Server
SMTP – Simple Mail Transfer Protocol
SNMP – Simple Network Management Protocol
SPAP – Shiva Password Authentication Protocol

T

TCP/IP – Transmission Control Protocol/Internet Protocol
TGS – Ticket Granting Service
TGT – Ticket Granting Ticket

U

UDP – User Datagram Protocol
URL – Uniform Resource Locator

V

VPN – virtual private network

W

WINS – Windows Internet Naming Service
WWW – World Wide Web